# SCOTLAND

CW00456427

| | | |
|---|---|---|
| Key to Map Pages | 2-3 | Town Plans ... 07 |
| Road Maps | 4-101 | Index to Town ... 20 |

## REFERENCE

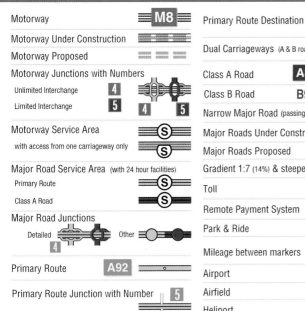

Motorway — M8

Motorway Under Construction

Motorway Proposed

Motorway Junctions with Numbers

Unlimited Interchange — 4

Limited Interchange — 5 / 4 / 5

Motorway Service Area — Ⓢ

with access from one carriageway only — Ⓢ

Major Road Service Area (with 24 hour facilities)

Primary Route — Ⓢ

Class A Road — Ⓢ

Major Road Junctions

Detailed / Other

4

Primary Route — A92

Primary Route Junction with Number — 5

Primary Route Destination — OBAN

Dual Carriageways (A & B roads)

Class A Road — A814

Class B Road — B9080

Narrow Major Road (passing places)

Major Roads Under Construction

Major Roads Proposed

Gradient 1:7 (14%) & steeper — » »

Toll — Toll |

Remote Payment System — Ⓒ

Park & Ride — P+R

Mileage between markers — 8

Airport — ✈

Airfield — ✝

Heliport — Ⓗ

(vehicular, sea) / (vehicular, river) / (foot only)

Railway and Station

Level Crossing and Tunnel

River or Canal

County or Unitary Authority Boundary

National Boundary

Built-up Area

Town, Village or Hamlet — ⊙

Wooded Area

Spot Height in Feet — 813 ·

Relief above 400' (122m)

National Grid Reference (kilometres) — 8 00

Area covered by Town Plan — SEE PAGE 102

## TOURIST INFORMATION

Abbey, Church, Friary, Priory — ✝

Animal Collection — 👣

Aquarium — 🐟

Arboretum, Botanical Garden — ♣

Aviary, Bird Garden — 🐦

Battle Site and Date — 1066 ✗

Blue Flag Beach — ▣

Bridge — ⌂

Castle (open to public) — 🏰

Castle with Garden (open to public) — 🏰

Cathedral — ✝

Cidermaker — 🍾

Country Park — Ψ

Distillery — 🍶

Farm Park, Open Farm — 🐖

Fortress, Hill Fort — ✳

Garden (open to public) — ✳

Golf Course — ⚐

Historic Building (open to public) — 🏛

Historic Building with Garden (open to public) — 🏛

Horse Racecourse — 🏇

Industrial Monument — ✿

Leisure Park, Leisure Pool — ⑤

Lighthouse — 🗼

Mine, Cave — ⛏

Monument — ♟

Motor Racing Circuit — 🏁

Museum, Art Gallery — Ⓜ

National Park

National Trust Property

Natural Attraction — ★

Nature Reserve or Bird Sanctuary — 🦅

Nature Trail or Forest Walk — 🍂

Picnic Site — 🌲

Place of Interest — Craft Centre •

Prehistoric Monument — 🗿

Railway, Steam or Narrow Gauge — 🚂

Roman Remains — 🏛

Theme Park — 🎡

Tourist Information Centre — 🅸

Viewpoint (360 degrees) — ☀

(180 degrees) — ☀

Vineyard — 🍇

Visitor Information Centre — Ⓥ

Wildlife Park — Ψ

Windmill — 🗙

Zoo or Safari Park — 🐘

## SCALE

0 1 2 3 4 5 ... 10 miles
0 1 2 3 4 5 ... 10 ... 16 kilometres

Map Pages 4-90
1:221,760
3.5 miles to 1 inch

EDITION 3 2020
Copyright © Geographers' A-Z Map Co. Ltd.

Contains Ordnance Survey data © Crown copyright and database right 2019

Base Relief by Geo-Innovations, © www.geoinnovations.co.uk
The Shopmobility logo is a registered symbol of The National Federation of Shopmobility.

A-Z
registered trade marks of Geographers' A-Z Map Company Ltd
www./az.co.uk

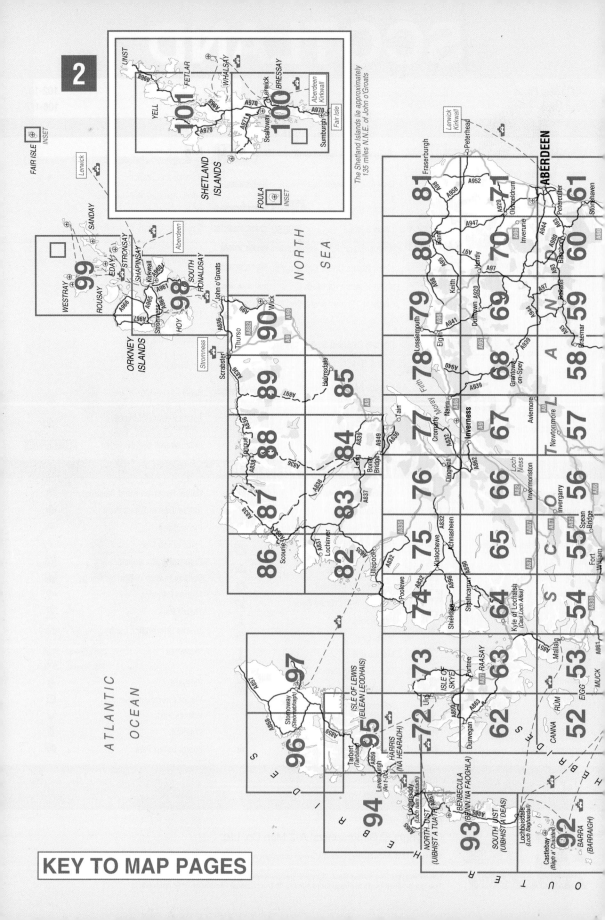

**KEY TO MAP PAGES**

2

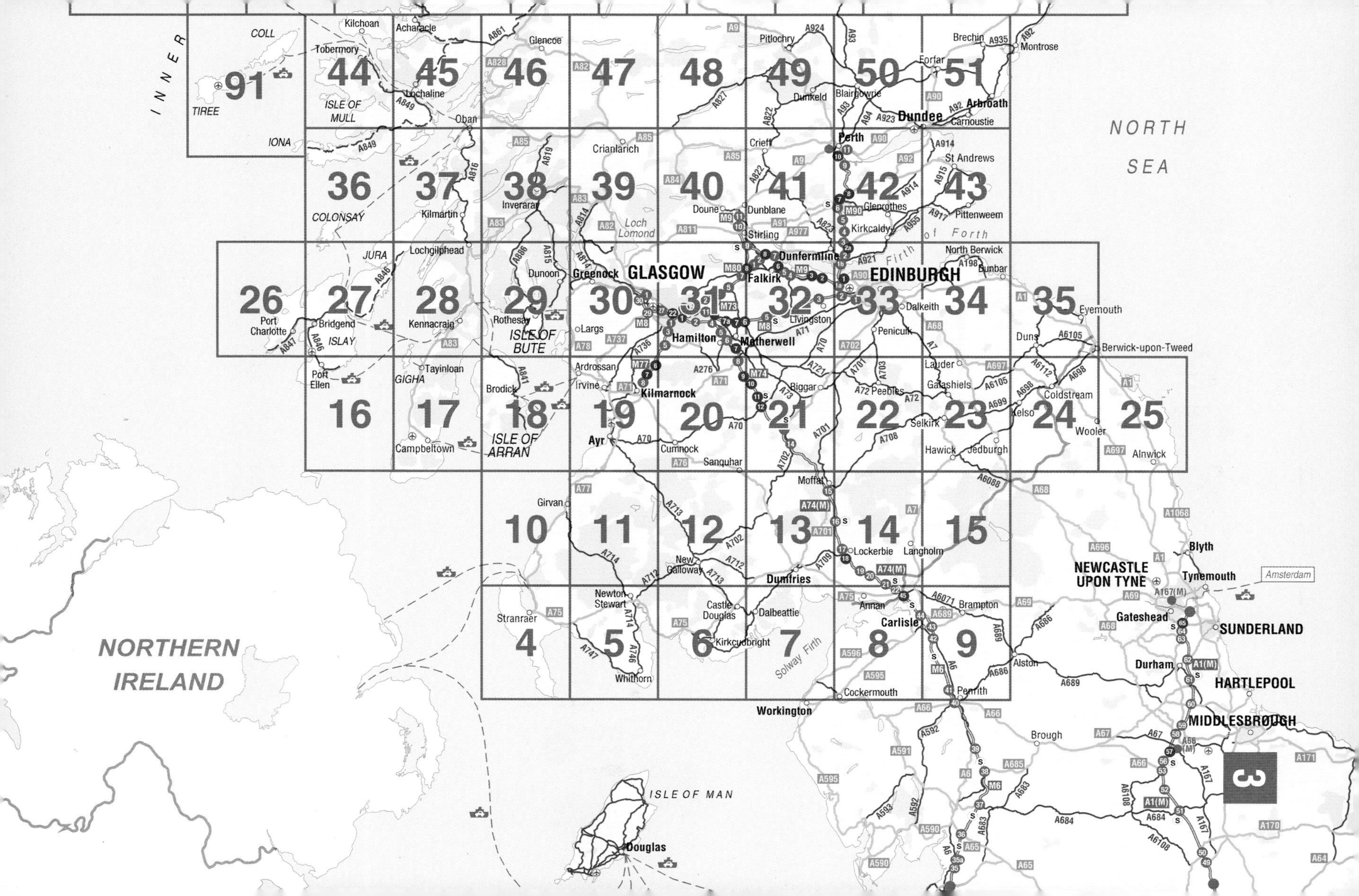

NORTH SEA

NORTH
SEA

INNER

COLL
TIREE
91

IONA
ISLE OF MULL
Kilchoan
Tobermory
44
Achacalle
Luchaline
45
Oban
A816
36
COLONSAY
JURA
27
ISLAY
16
Port Ellen
Port Charlotte
26

Kilmartin
37
Kennacraig
28
Lochgilphead
Tarbert
GIGHA
17
Campbeltown

Inveraray
38
Dunoon
29
ISLE OF BUTE
Rothesay
18
Brodick
ISLE OF ARRAN

Criahlarich
47
Loch Lomond
39
Largs
30
Ardrossan
Irvine
19
Ayr
20
Girvan
10
Stranraer
4

Glencoe
46

Pitlochry
Dunkeld
49
Crieff
41
Dunblane
Doune
Stirling
40
GLASGOW
Greenock
31
Hamilton
Motherwell
32
Kilmarnock
Cumnock
Sanquhar
21
New Galloway
11
Newton Stewart
5
Whithorn

Montrose
Brechin
Forfar
50
Blairgowrie
Perth
42
Glenrothes
Kirkcaldy
Dunfermline
EDINBURGH
33
Peebles
22
Moffat
13
Dumfries
12
Castle Douglas
Dalbeattie
6
Kirkcudbright
7

Arbroath
Carnoustie
51
St Andrews
Dundee
43
Pittenweem
Firth of Forth
34
Dalkeith
Penicuik
Galashiels
Selkirk
23
Hawick
Langholm
14
Lockerbie
Annan
Carlisle
8
Cockermouth
Workington
Solway Firth

35
Eyemouth
North Berwick
Dunbar
Berwick-upon-Tweed
Duns
Coldstream
Kelso
24
Jedburgh
15
Brampton
Penrith
9

Alnwick
Wooler
25

Blyth
Tynemouth
NEWCASTLE UPON TYNE
Gateshead
SUNDERLAND
Durham
HARTLEPOOL
MIDDLESBROUGH
Brough

Amsterdam

ISLE OF MAN
Douglas

NORTHERN IRELAND

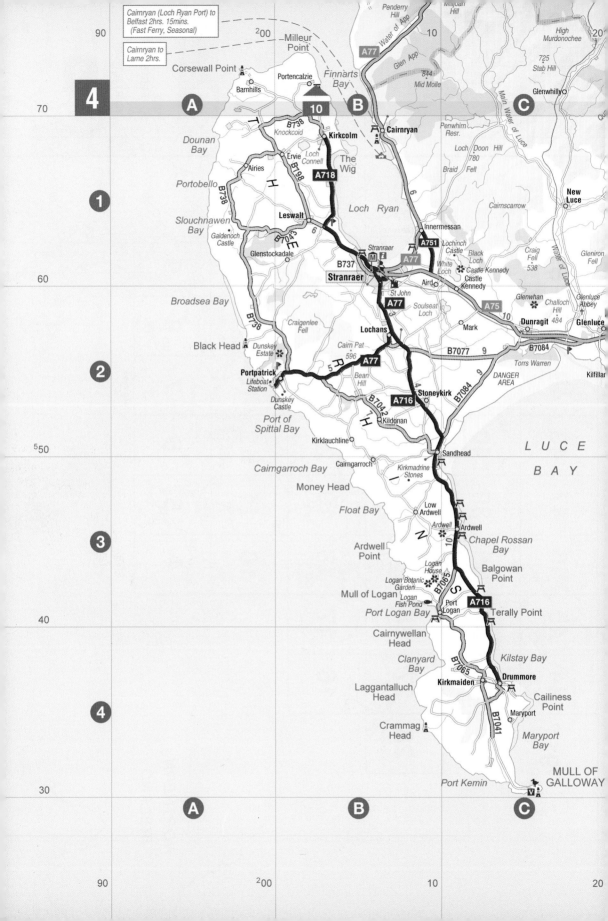

Cairnryan (Loch Ryan Port) to Belfast 2hrs. 15mins. (Fast Ferry, Seasonal)

Cairnryan to Larne 2hrs.

90 200 —Milleur Point

Corsewall Point

Portencalzie

Finnarts Bay

A77 Water of App

Penderry Hill

Mill Oah Hill

High Murdonochee

10

20 Glen App

834 Mid Moile

725 Stab Hill

Glenwhilly

70 A 10 B 10 C

Barnhills

Kirkcolm

Cairnryan

Penwhirn Resr.

Dounan Bay

B7738

Knockcoid

The Wig

Loch Doon Hill 780

New Luce

Airies

Ervie

Loch Connell

A718

6

Braid Fell

Cairnscarrow

1

Portobello

B7738

B198

Loch Ryan

Innermessan

A751

Lochinch Castle

Black Loch

Craig Fell 538

Gleniron Fell

Slouchnawen Bay

Galdenoch Castle

Leswalt

6

Stranraer

A77

White Loch

Castle Kennedy

Glenstockadale

B737

Stranraer

Aird

Castle Kennedy

Glenwhan Gardens

Challoch

Glenluce Abbey

60 St John

A77

Soulseat Loch

Mark

A75

10

Dunragit 484

Glenluce

Broadsea Bay

B7738

Craigenlee Fell

Lochans

B7077

9

Torrs Warren

B7084

Black Head

Dunskey Estate

Cairn Pat 596

A77

DANGER AREA

Kilfillar

2

Portpatrick
Lifeboat Station

5

Bean Hill

A77

B7084

9

Dunskey Castle

B7042

A716

Stoneykirk

Kildonan

Port of Spittal Bay

Kirklauchline

Sandhead

L U C E

50 Cairngarroch Bay

Cairngarroch

Kirkmadrine Stones

B A Y

Money Head

Float Bay

Low Ardwell

Ardwell

Chapel Rossan Bay

3

Ardwell Point

Ardwell

10

Ardwell Point

Logan House

N

Balgowan Point

Logan Botanic Garden

B7065

S

Mull of Logan

Logan Fish Pond

Port Logan

A716

Terally Point

Port Logan Bay

40

Cairnywellan Head

Clanyard Bay

B7065

Kilstay Bay

Laggantalluch Head

Kirkmaiden

Drummore

Cailiness Point

4

Crammag Head

Maryport

B7041

Maryport Bay

MULL OF GALLOWAY

30 Port Kemin

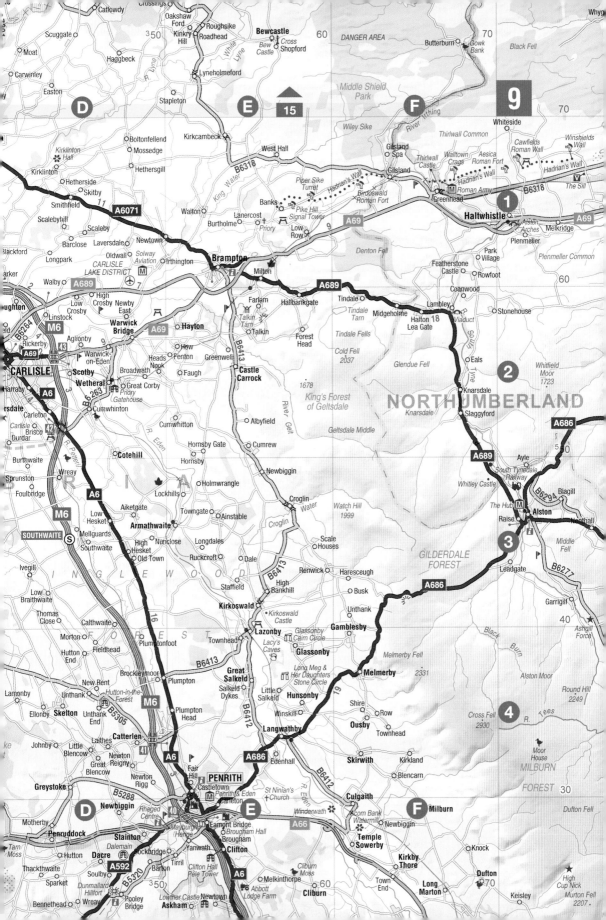

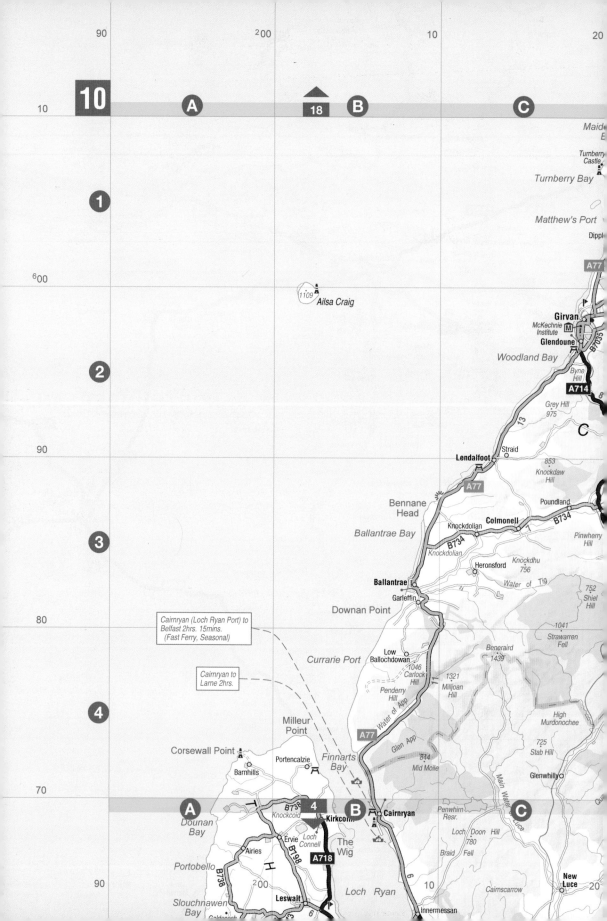

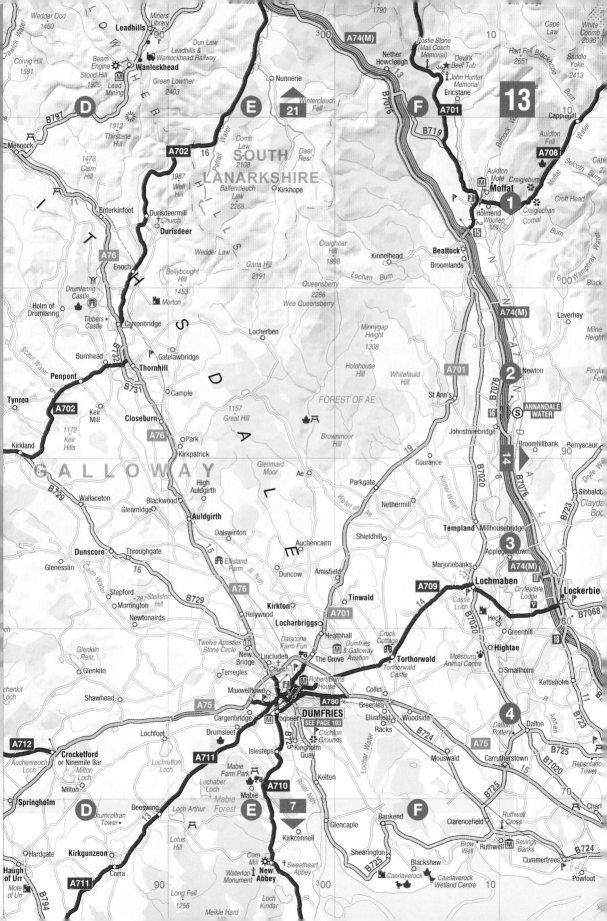

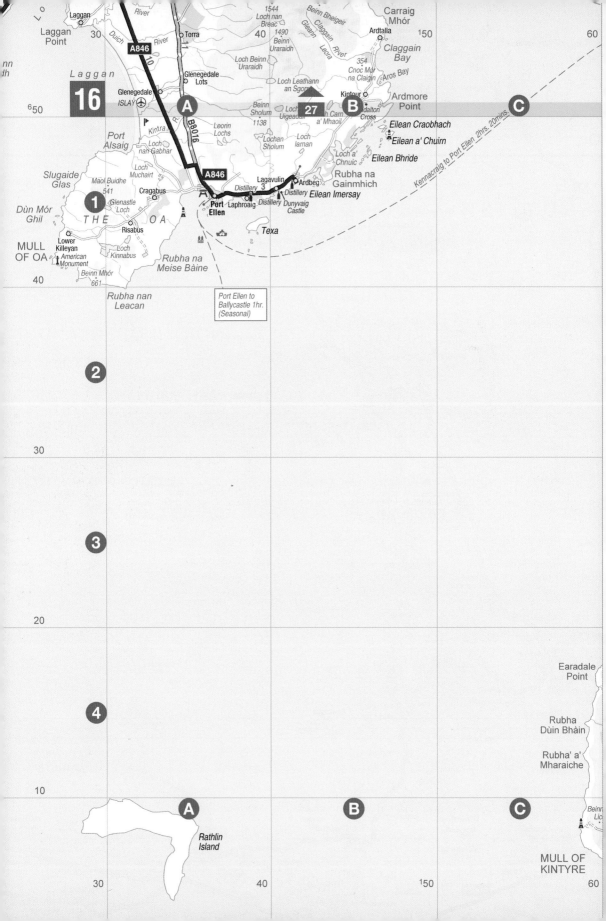

Laggan

**16**

Lo

Laggan

Laggan Point

30

Duich River

A846

10

11

Torra

River

Glenegedale Lots

Glenegedale
ISLAY

B8016

A

1544
Loch nan
Breac

40

1490
Beinn
Uraraidh

Loch Beinn
Uraraidh

Loch Leathann
an Sgorra

Beinn
Sholum
1138

Loch
Uigeadail

Loch
Sholum

Loch
Iarnan

Lochan
Sholum

Leorin
Lochs

Kintra

R.

Port Alsaig

Loch
nan Gabhar

Loch
Muchairt

Slugaide
Glas

Maol Buidhe
541

Cragabus

Glenastle
Loch

Dùn Mór
Ghil

THE        OA

Risabus

MULL
OF OA

Lower
Killeyan

American
Monument

Loch
Kinnabus

Beinn Mhór
661

40

Rubha na
Meise Bàine

Rubha nan
Leacan

1544
Beinn Bheigeir

Carraig
Mhór

Ardtalla

150

Claggain
Bay

Claggain River

Gleann Leora

354
Cnoc Mór
na Claigin

Kintour

Aros Bay

Ardmore
Point

A

27

B

dalton
Cross

Eilean Craobhach

Eilean a' Chuirn

Eilean Bhride

Loch a'
Chnuic

Rubha na
Gainmhich

Loch a'
Chnuic

Distillery

Lagavulin

3

Ardbeg

Distillery

Eilean Imersay

Distillery

Dunyvaig
Castle

Port
Ellen

Laphroaig

A846

Texa

Kennacraig to Port Ellen 2hrs. 20mins.

60

50

6 50

Port Ellen to
Ballycastle 1hr.
(Seasonal)

2

30

3

20

Earadale
Point

Rubha
Dùin Bhàin

Rubha' a'
Mharaiche

4

10

A

Rathlin
Island

B

C

Beinn
Lic

MULL OF
KINTYRE

30

40

150

60

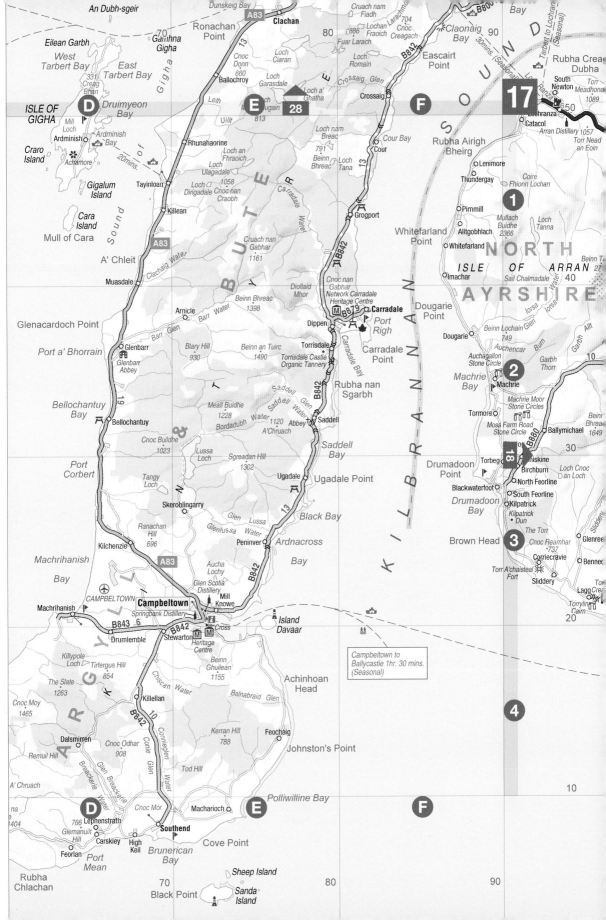

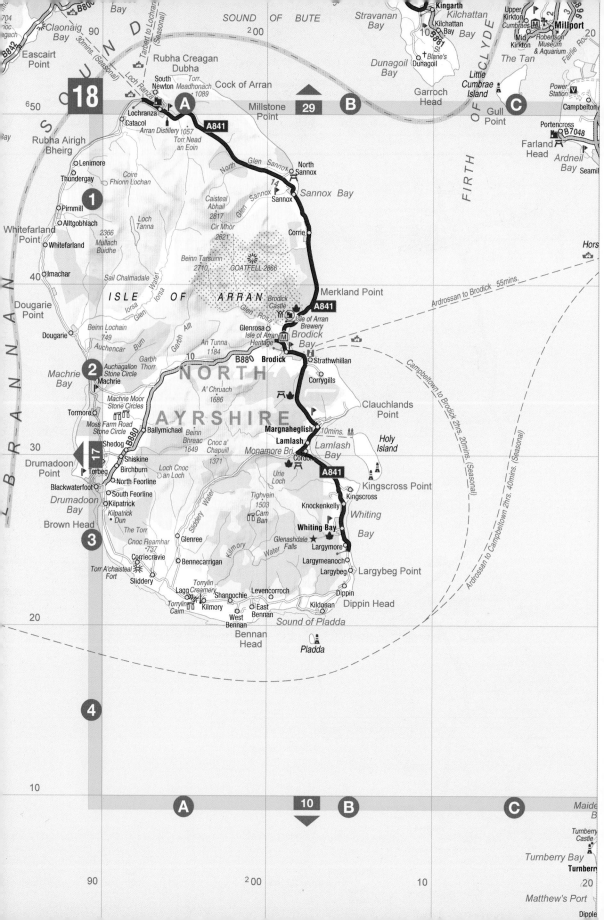

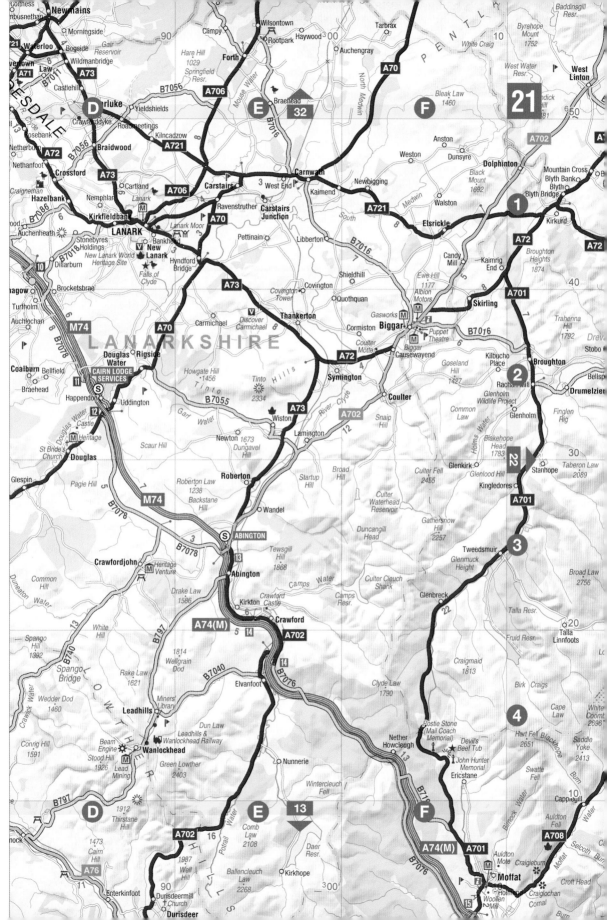

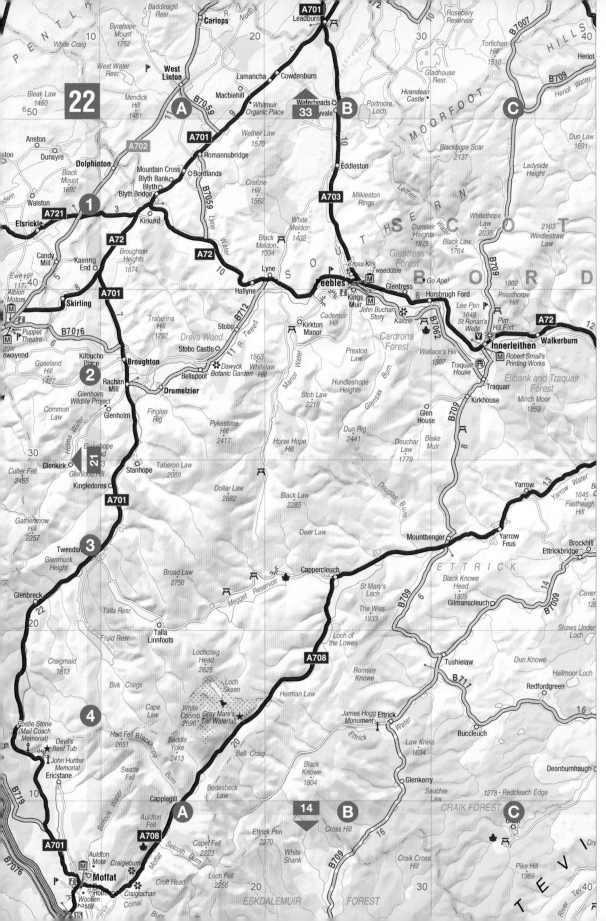

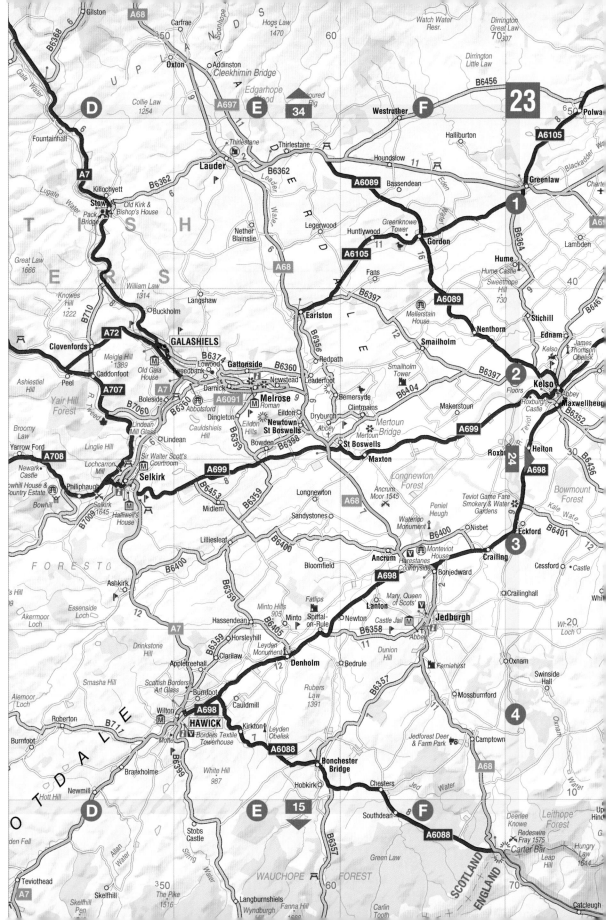

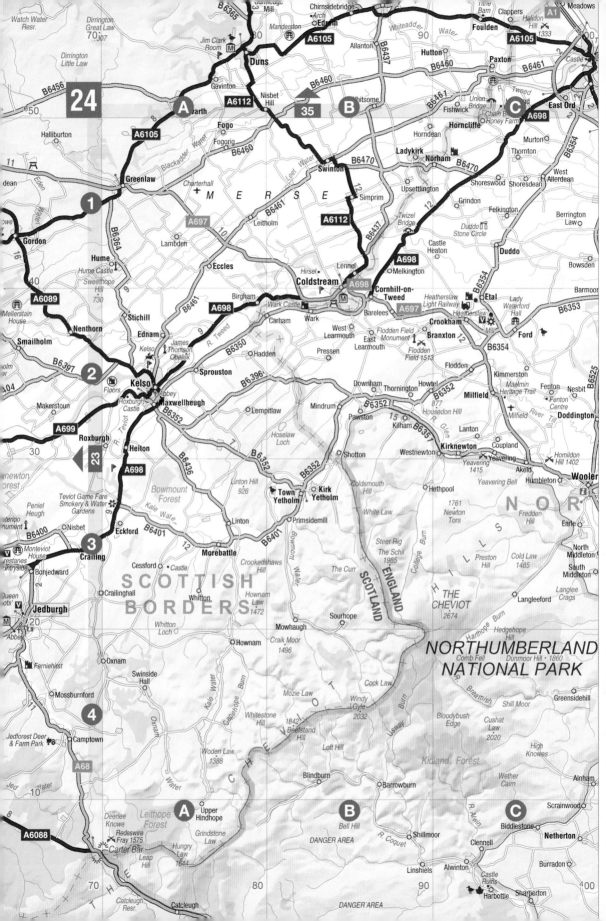

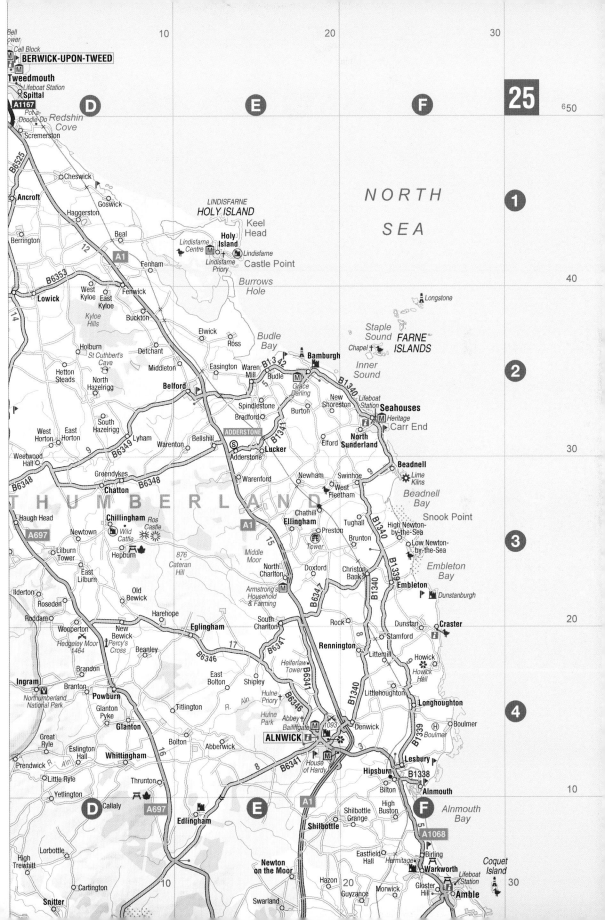

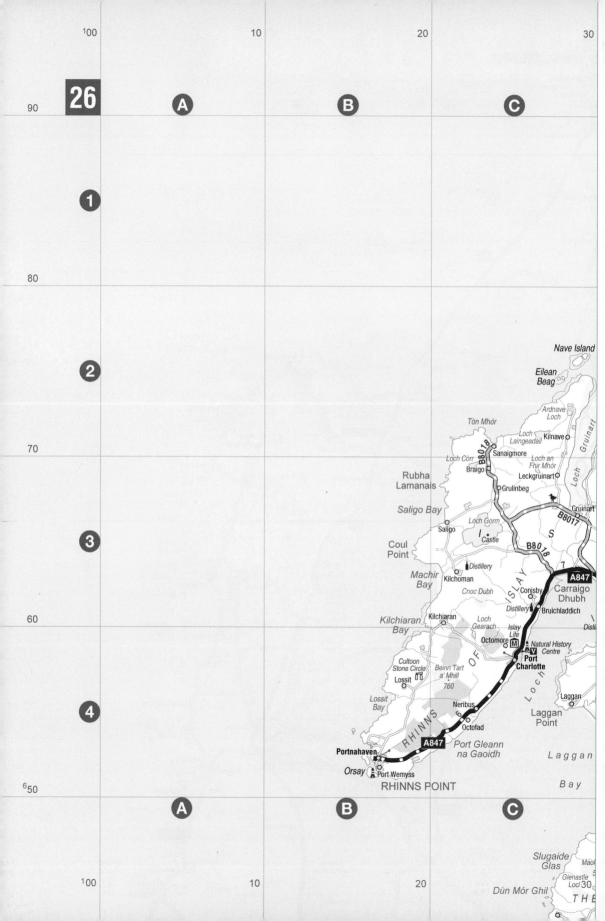

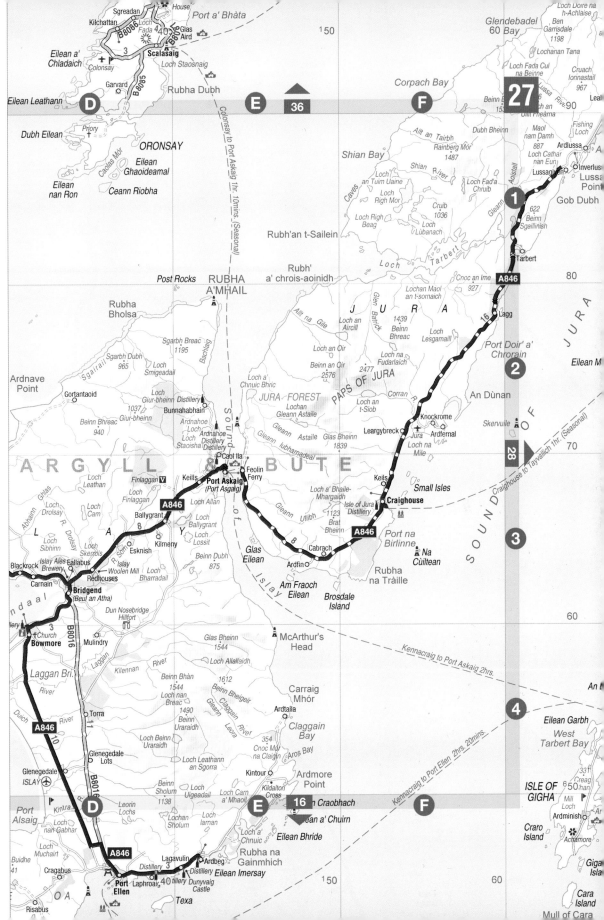

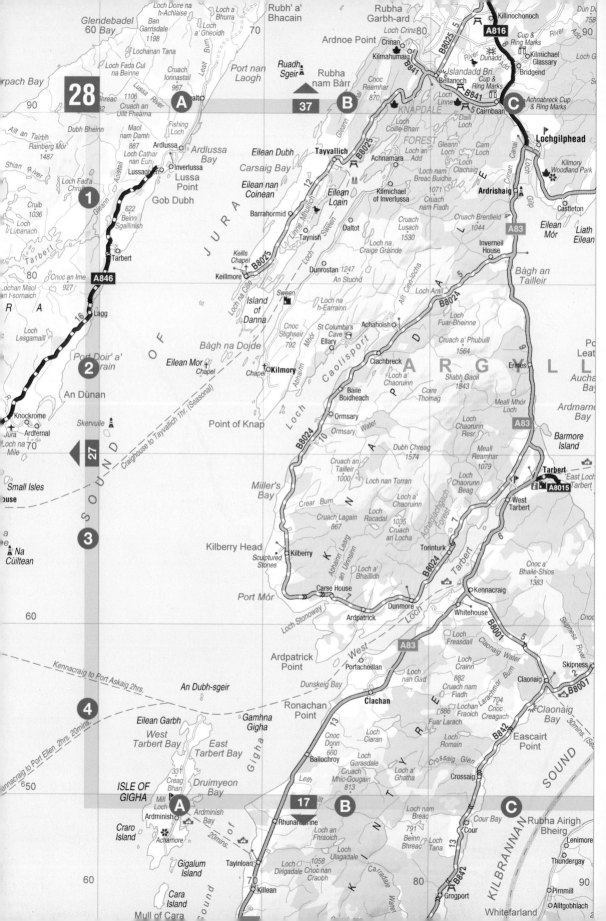

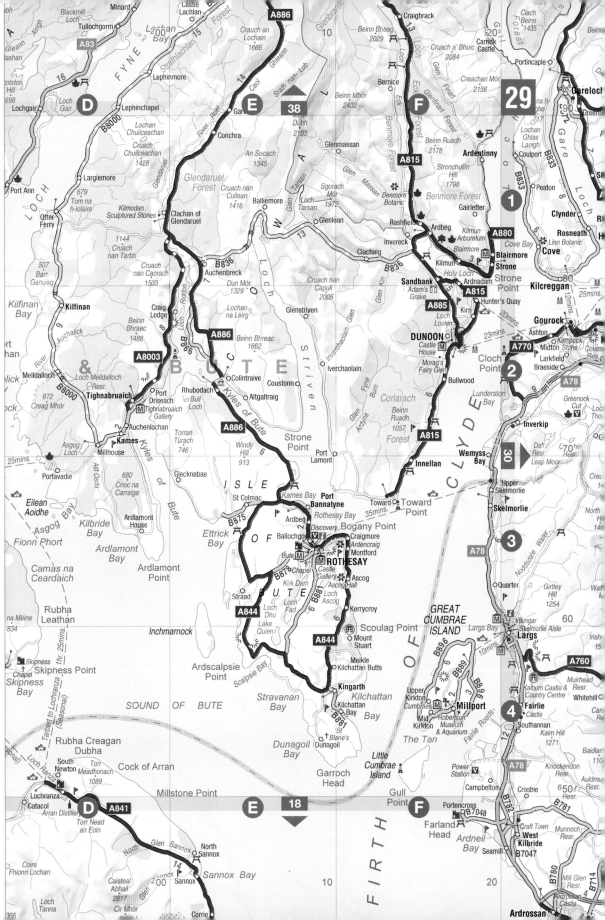

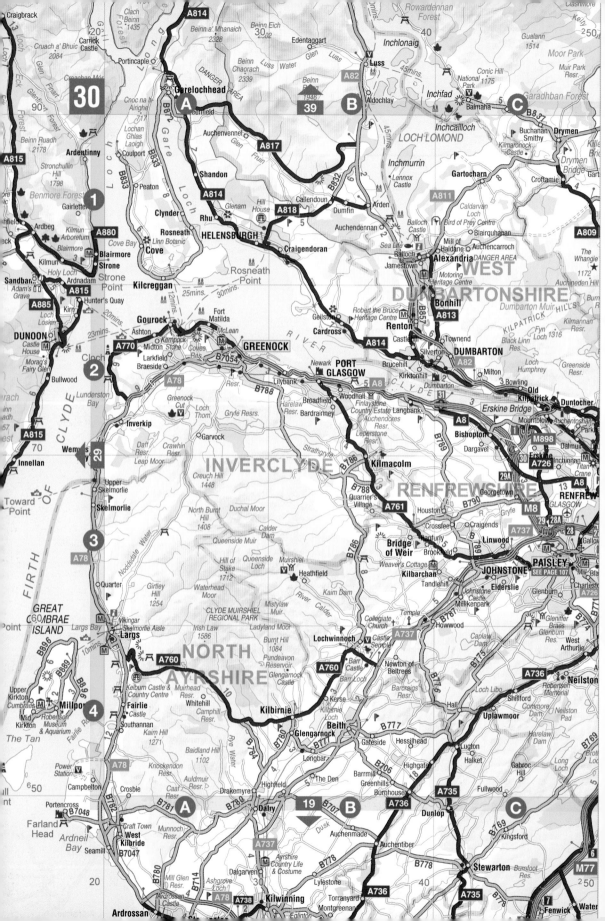

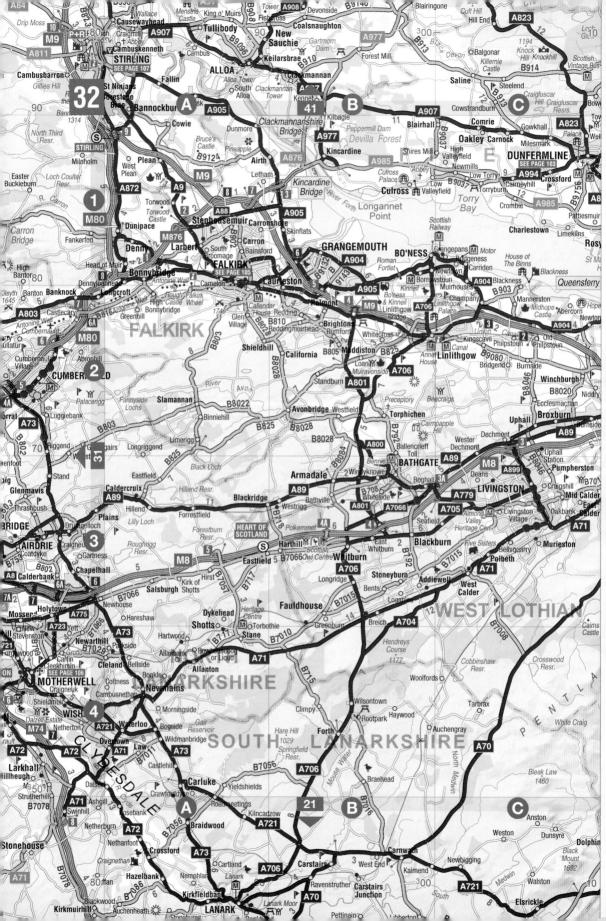

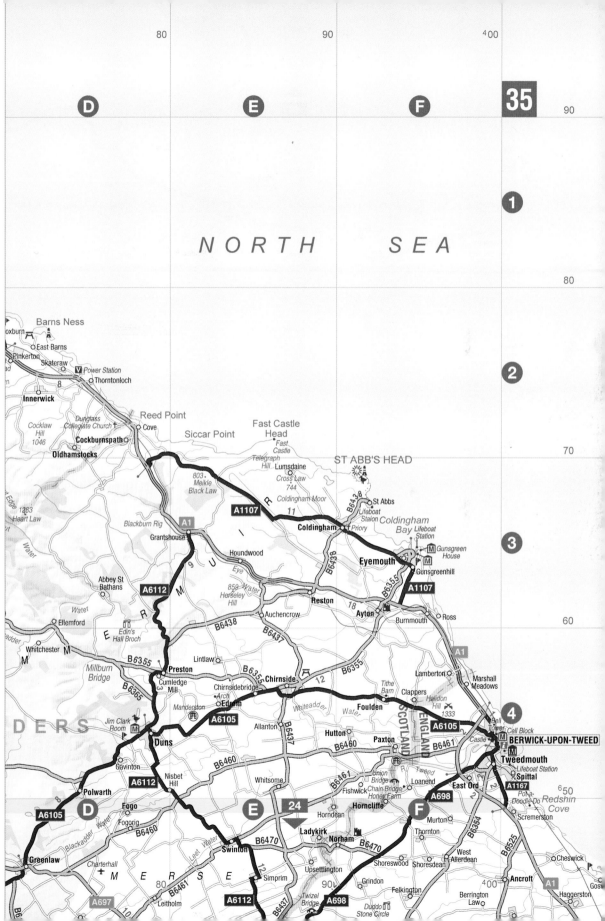

NORTH    SEA

Barns Ness
oxburn
East Barns
Pinkerton  Skateraw
V Power Station
Thorntonloch
Innerwick

Cocklaw
Hill
1046
Dunglass
Collegiate Church †
Reed Point
Cove
Siccar Point
Cockburnspath
Oldhamstocks

Fast Castle
Head
Fast
Castle
Telegraph
Hill  Lumsdaine
Cross Law
744
Coldingham Moor

ST ABB'S HEAD

803.
Meikle
Black Law
A1107
R
11
B6438
St Abbs
Lifeboat
Staion
Coldingham
Bay  Lifeboat
Station

A1
Grantshouse

Blackburn Rig

1283
Heart Law

Water

Houndwood

Eye

Coldingham  † Priory
Eyemouth
M Gunsgreen
House
Gunsgreenhill
A1107

Abbey St
Bathans
A6112

859
Herseley
Hill

Water

Water
Ellemford

Edin's
Hall Broch

Reston
Auchencrow
B6438
B6437

Ayton
Burnmouth
Ross

A1

Whitchester  M
M

B6355
Preston
B6365
Millburn
Bridge

Lintlaw

B6355
Chirnside

Cumledge
Mill
Chirnsidebridge
Arch
Manderston
Edrom

12
B6355
Tithe
Barn
Clappers
Halidon
Hill
1333

Lamberton
Marshall
Meadows

A1

Whiteadder  Water
Foulden
A6105

DERS
Jim Clark
Room  M
Duns

Allanton
Hutton
Paxton
B6460
SCOTLAND  ENGLAND
A6105
Bell
Tower  Cell Block
M BERWICK-UPON-TWEED

Gavinton
A6112  Nisbet
Hill
Whitsome

B6461
B6460
Union
Bridge
Fishwick
Chain Bridge
Honey Farm
Tweed
Loanend
East Ord
A698

Castle
M Tweedmouth
Lifeboat Station
Spittal
A1167

Polwarth
A6105  D
Fogo
Fogorig
B6460
Whitsome

E
24
▼
Ladykirk
Norham
B6470
Horncliffe

F
Murton
Thornton
B6354

Pota-
Doodle-Do Redshin
Cove
Scremerston

Greenlaw
Charterhall
M  MERSE
Swinton
B6470
Horndean

Upsettlington
Simprim
Grindon
Felkington

Shoreswood  Shoresdean
West
Allerdean
Berrington
Law

Cheswick

A1167
Ancroft
A1
Gos

A697
Leitholm
A6112
Twizel
Bridge
A698
Duddo
Stone Circle
Haggerston

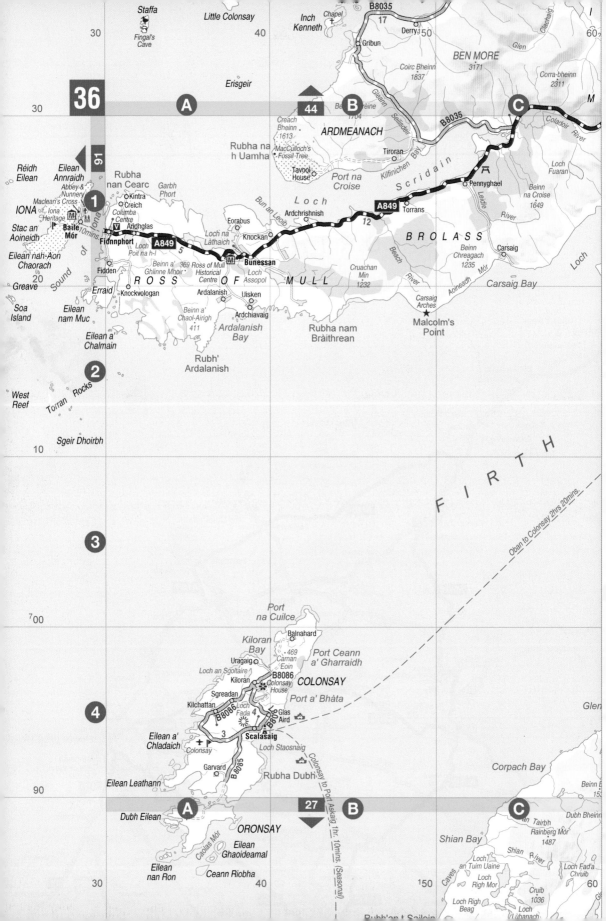

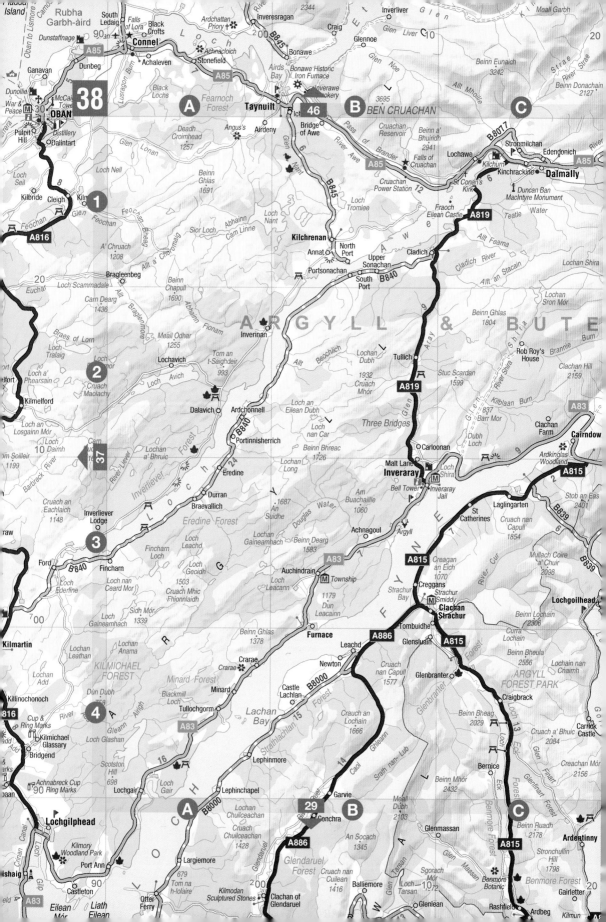

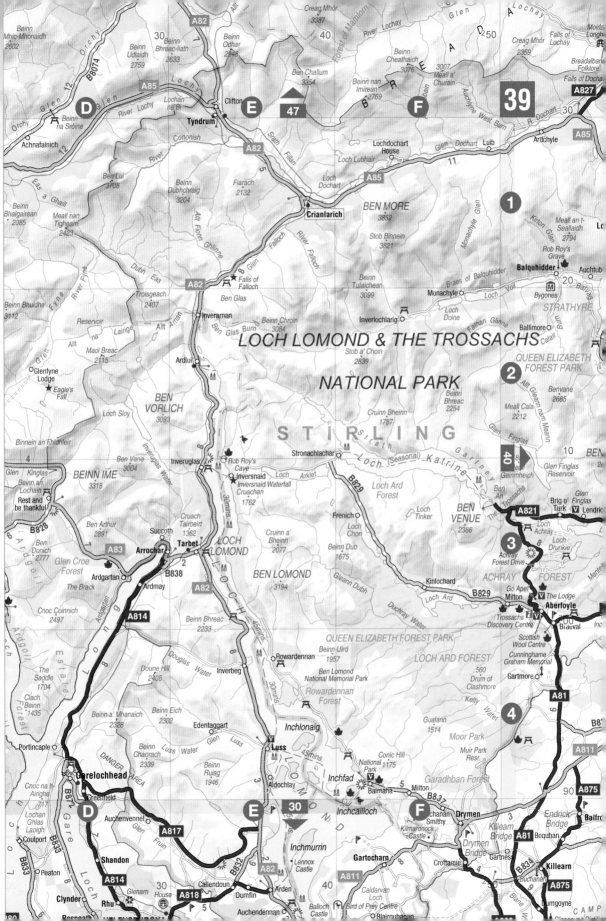

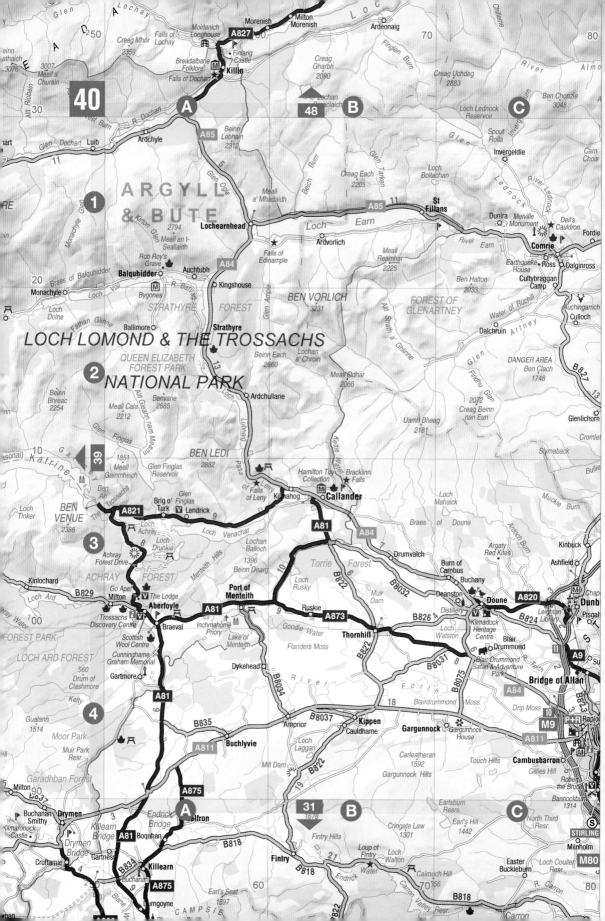

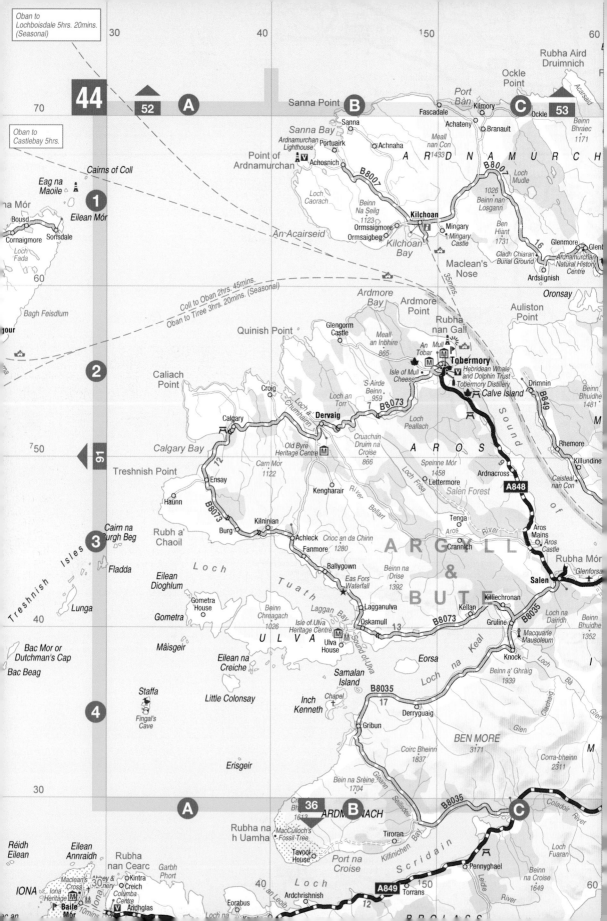

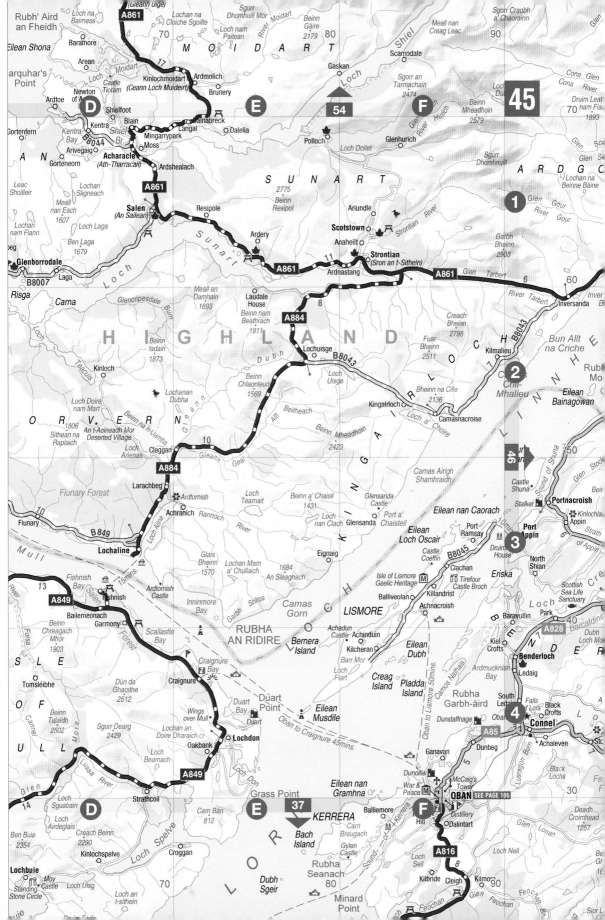

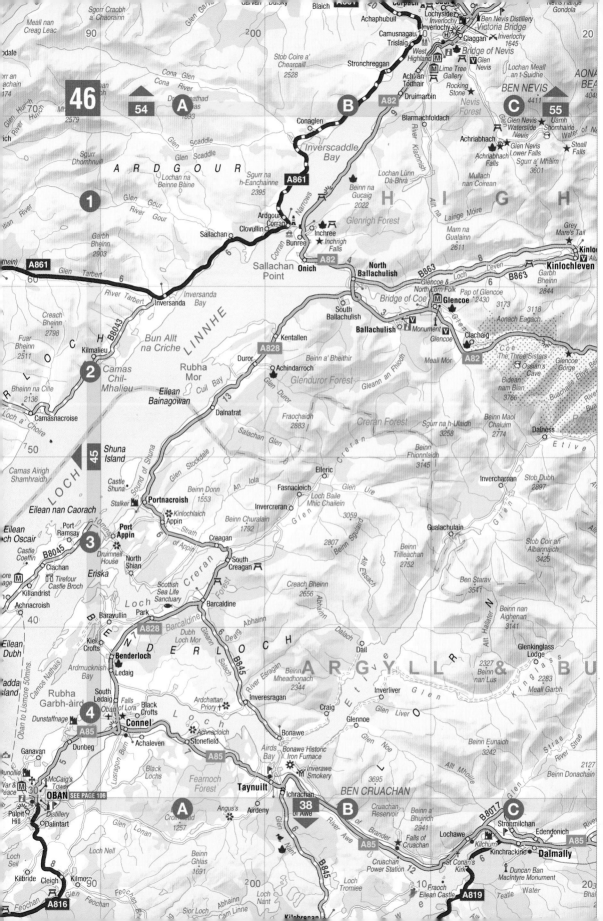

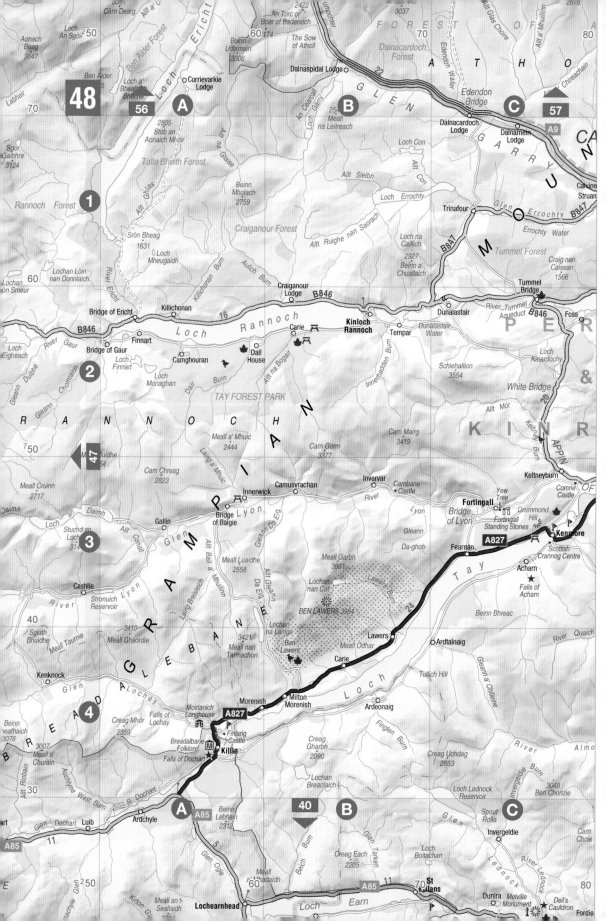

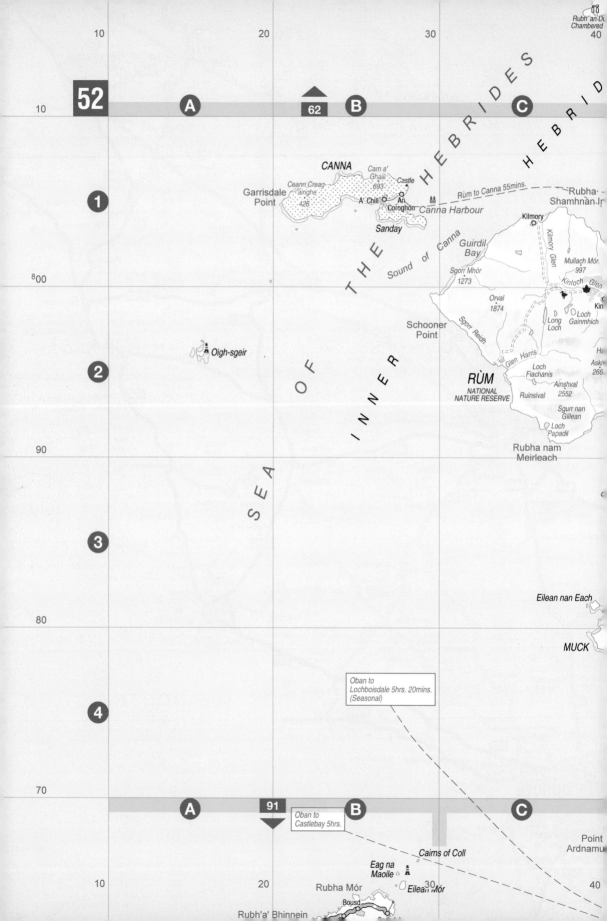

10

Rubh' an Du
Chambered

**1**

CANNA

Garrisdale
Point

Ceann Creag-
airighe
426

Carn a'
Ghaili
693

Castle

A' Chill

An
Coroghon

Canna Harbour

Sanday

Sound of Canna

Rùm to Canna 55mins.

Rubha
Shamhnàn.I

Kilmory

Kilmory Glen

Mullach Mór
997

Kinloch Glen

Kin

Guirdil
Bay

Sgorr Mhór
1273

Schooner
Point

Orval
1874

Sgorr Reidh

Long
Loch

Loch
Gainmhich

Loch
Fiachanis

Ha

Aski
266

8'00

0

Oigh-sgeir

**2**

SEA

OF

THE

INNER

**RÙM**
NATIONAL
NATURE RESERVE

Glen Harris

Ruinsival

Ainshval
2552

Sgurr nan
Gillean

Loch
Papadil

Rubha nam
Meirleach

90

**3**

Eilean nan Each

80

MUCK

Oban to
Lochboisdale 5hrs. 20mins.
(Seasonal)

**4**

70

Oban to
Castlebay 5hrs.

Point
Ardnamu

Cairns of Coll

10    20    30    40

Eag na
Maoile

Rubha Mór

Eilean Mór

Rubh'a' Bhinnein

Bousd

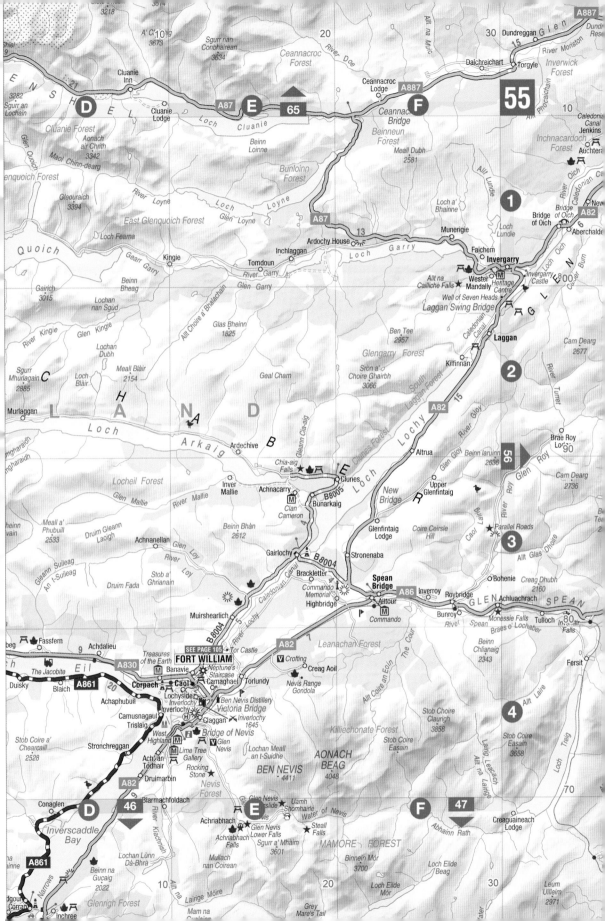

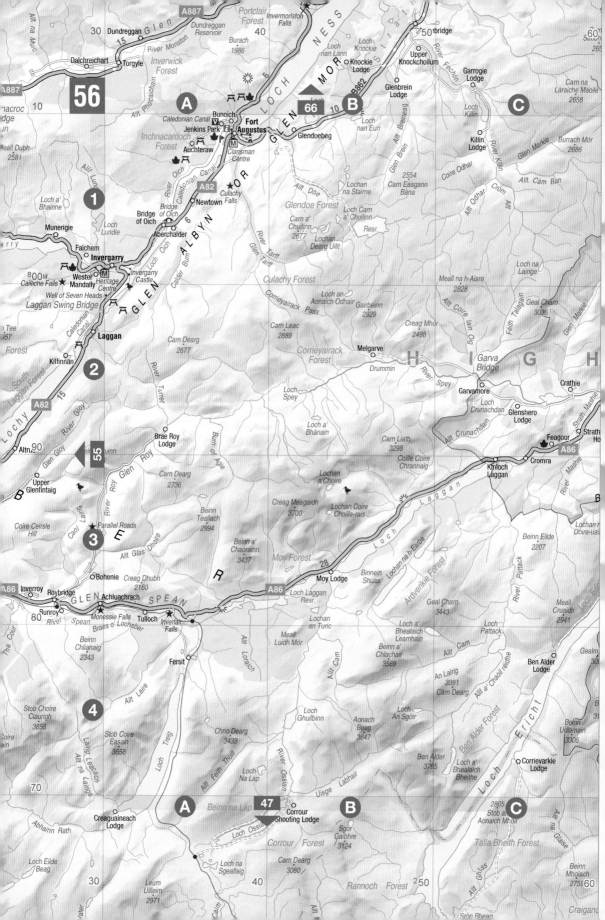

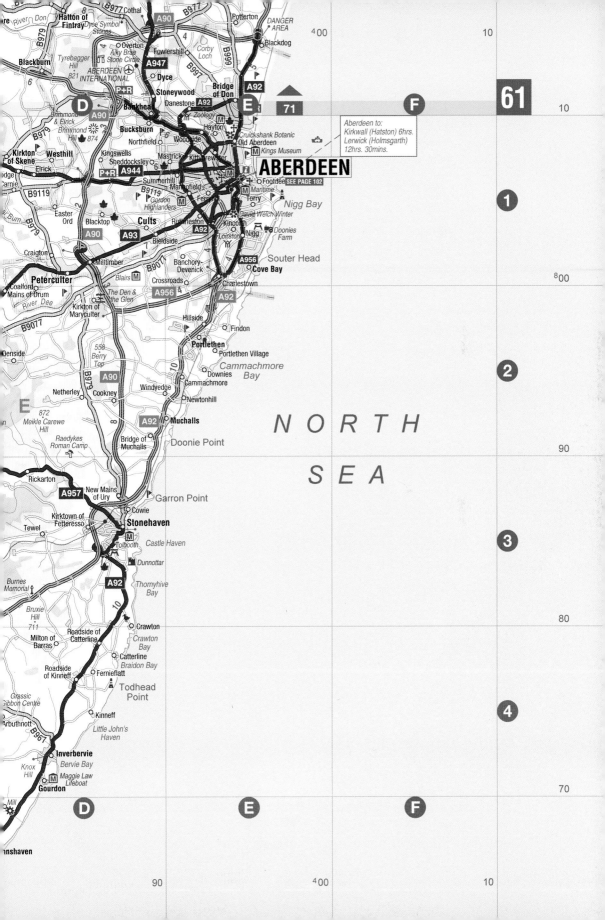

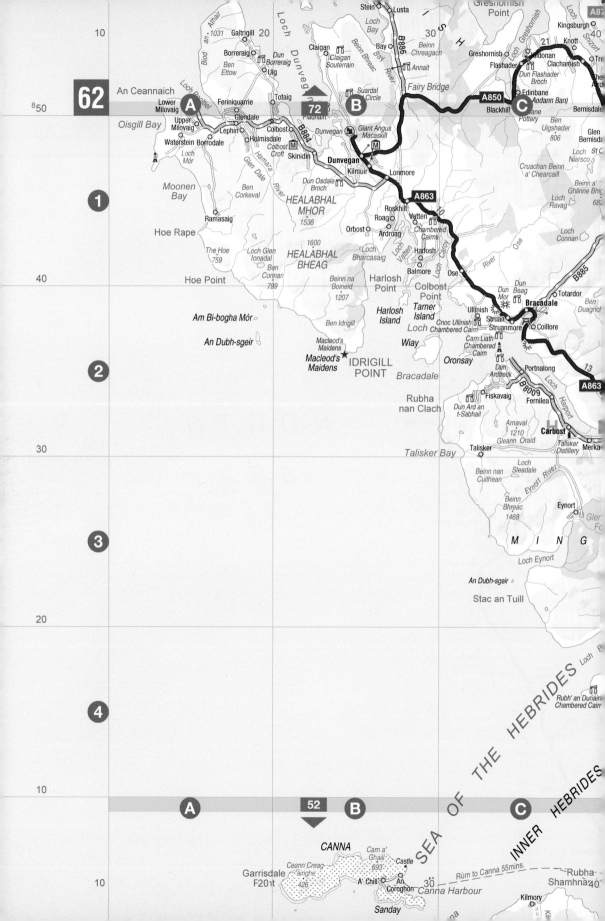

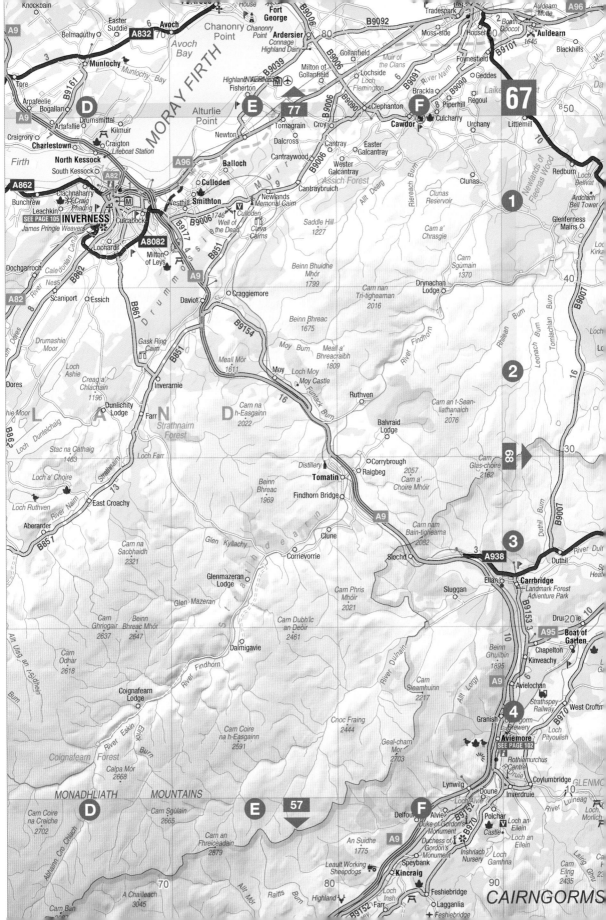

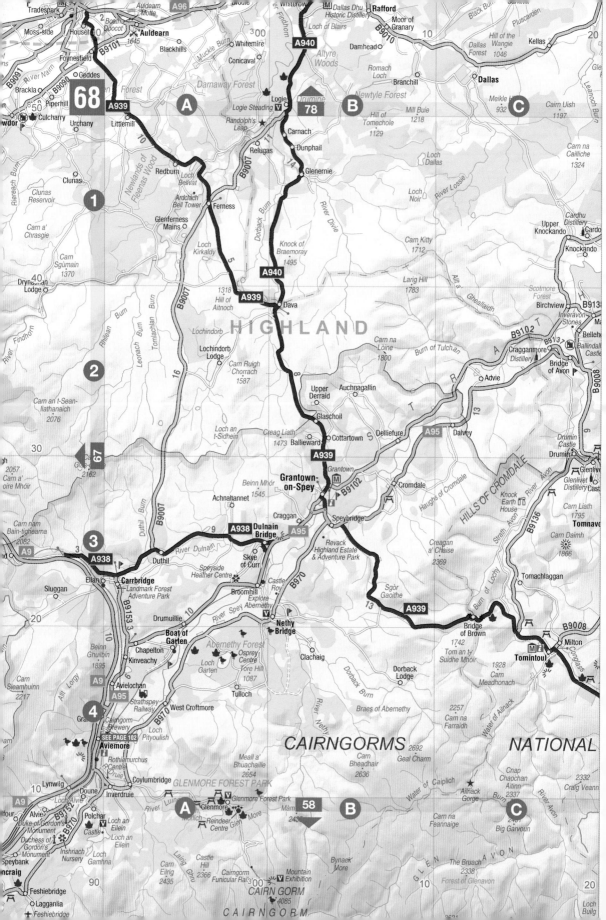

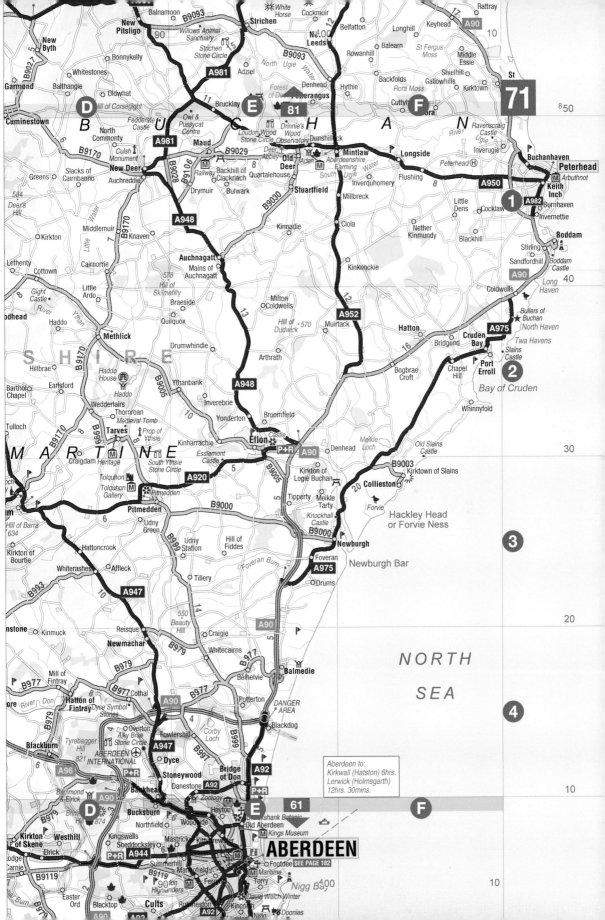

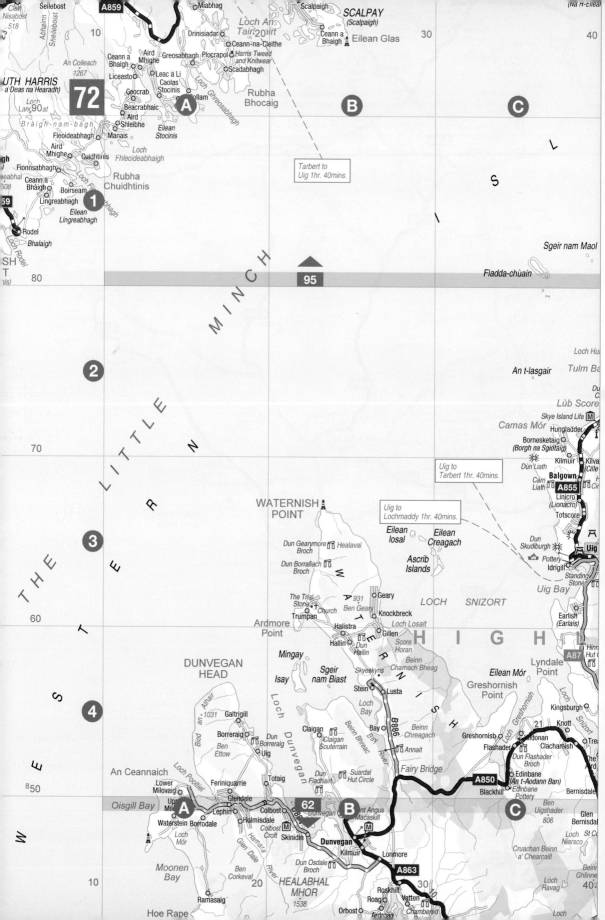

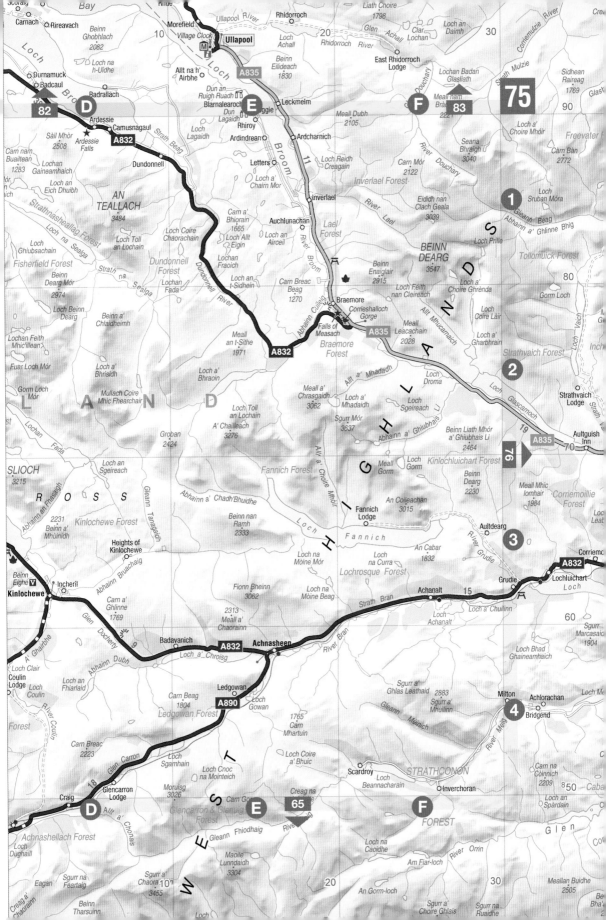

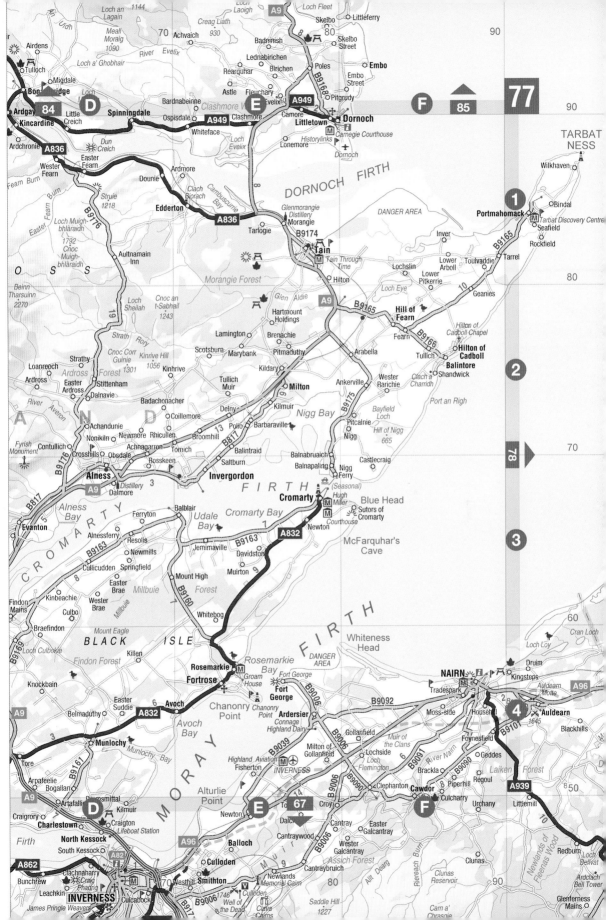

S E A

Fisheries & Community
Stotfield
Branderburgh
Seatown
B90 40
Lossiemouth
B9135
A941
Loch Spynie
Lossie Forest
Moray Motor
Spynie Palace
Bishopmill
Elgin
Ashgrove
New Elgin
Glassgreen
Linkwood
A941
Thornshill
Upper Bogside
Moss of Barmuckity
Clackmarras
Longmorn
Whitewreath
Millbuies
Coleburn
Pikey Hill 1164
Glen of Rothes
Rothes
A941
Cairn Cattoch 1210
Elchies Forest
Braehead
Archiestown
B9102
Robertstown
Macallan Distillery
Craigellachie
Speyside Cooperage

Urquhart Stone Circle
Lochhill
Sheriffston
Lhanbryde
Scotsburn
Cranloch
Loch na Bo
Crofts of Dipple
Baxters
Fochabers
Folk
Ordiquish
Inchberry
Teindland Forest
Teindland
Wood of Ordiequish
Orton
Auchroisk Distillery
Malcolmburn
Mulben
Ben Aigan 1546
Mount Pleasant
Hill of Towie 1111
Maggieknockater
Keith & Dufftown Railway (Whisky Line)
Towiemore
Drummuir
Tullich

DANGER AREA
Kingston
Garmouth
Spey Viaduct
Bogmoor
Tugnet Ice House
Scottish Dolphin Centre
Spey Bay
Nether Dallachy
Lower Dallachy
Upper Dallachy
Auchenreath
Porttannachy
Auchenhalrig
Newlands of Tynet
Mosstodloch
A96
Cowfords
B9015
Speymouth Forest
Whiteash Hill Wood
B9016
Forgie
A96
Aultmore
Broadrashes
B9014
Keith
Mains of Auchindachy
Glen of Coachford
Pitlurg Castle

Spey Bay

Buckpool
Portessie
Buckie
A990
A942
Portgordon
Slackhead
Broadley
Clochan
Drybridge
Shiel Muir
Aultmore
Deerhill
Grange Crossroads
Newmill
B9017
Fife Keith
Strathisla Distillery
A95
Nethermills
The Bin Forest
Upper Cuttlehill

B9021
Findochty
B9020
Bauds of Cullen
Findochty Castle
Rathven
A942
Bin of Cullen 1051
Ianstown

Portknockie
Cullen Bay
Seatown
Mercat Cross
Cullen
A98
Findlater Castle
Sandend
Logie Head
Milton
Kirktown of Deskford
Berryhillock
Joiner's Workshop
B9018
Mains of Edinpight
1028 Lurg Hill
Crannoch
Bracobrae
Sillyearn
Knock
Drumnagorrach
Farmtown
B9117
1412 Knock Hill
Drums of Park
Brodi
Ca350
Millt Roth
Ruthven
Corse of Kinnoir

30 40 50

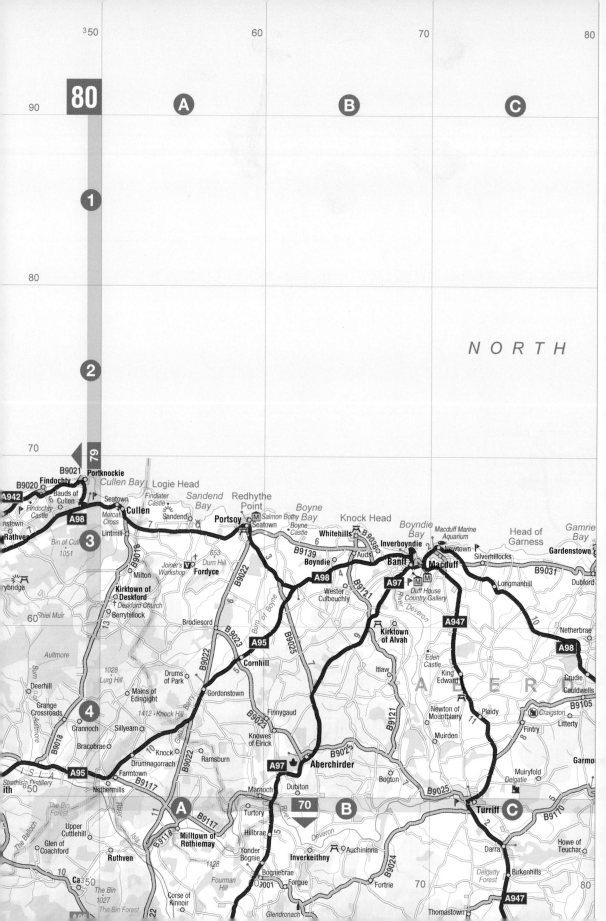

NORTH

**A**  **B**  **C**

90

1

80

2

70

79

B9021 **Portknockie**
B9020 **Findochty**
A942 Bauds of Cullen
Findochty Castle
**Rathven**  A98  Seatown  **Cullen**  Cullen Bay  Logie Head
Mercat Cross  Findlater Castle  Sandend Bay  Redhythe Point
Lintmill  7  Sandend  **Portsoy**  Seatown  Salmon Bothy Bay  Boyne Bay  Knock Head  Boyndie Bay
Bin of Cullen 1051  **3**  653  Durn Hill  Boyne Castle  6  Whitehills  Inverboyndie  Macduff Marine Aquarium  Head of Garness  Gamrie Bay
Joiner's Workshop  **Fordyce**  B9139  **Boyndie**  Auds  **Banff**  **Macduff**  Newtyon  Silverhillocks  **Gardenstown**
Milton  **Kirktown of Deskford**  Deskford Church  A98  Wester Culbeuchly  B9121  A97  Duff House Country Gallery  B9031  Dubford
Berryhillock  13  Brodiesord  B9023  A95  B9025  **Kirktown of Alvah**  Deveron  A947  Netherbrae  A98
Shiel Muir  60  Bin of Boyne  3  Eden Castle  10  Crudie  Cauldwells
Aultmore  1028 Lurg Hill  Drums of Park  5  Cornhill  7  Itlaw  King Edward  B9105
Deerhill  1412 · Knock Hill  Gordonstown  Finnygaud  B9121  Newton of Mountblairy  11  Plaidy  Craigston  Litterty
**Grange Crossroads**  **4**  Mains of Edingight  B9023  Knowes of Elrick  Muirden  Fintry  **Garmo**
Crannoch  Sillyearn  A97  **Aberchirder**  B9025  Bogton  Muiryfold Delgatie  **Garmo**
Bracobrae  10  Knock  Ramsburn  B9025  **Turriff**  B9170
A95  Drumnagorrach  B9022  **Turriff**  B9170
Strathisla Distillery  Farmtown  Marnoch  Dubiton  B9025  **Turriff**
**ith**  50  Nethermills  B9117  Turtory  Deveron  Darra  Howe of Teuchar
The Bin Forest  **A**  B9117  Hillbrae  **70**  **B**  B9024  Delgatty Forest  Birkenhills
Upper Cuttlehill  **Milltown of Rothiemay**  Yonder Bognie  **Inverkeithny**  Auchininna  A947
Glen of Coachford  Ruthven  1128  Bogniebrae  Forgue  B9001  Fortrie  70  A947
10  Ca 350  The Bin 1027  Fourman Hill  Glendronach  Thomastown
The Bin Forest  Corse of Kinnoir

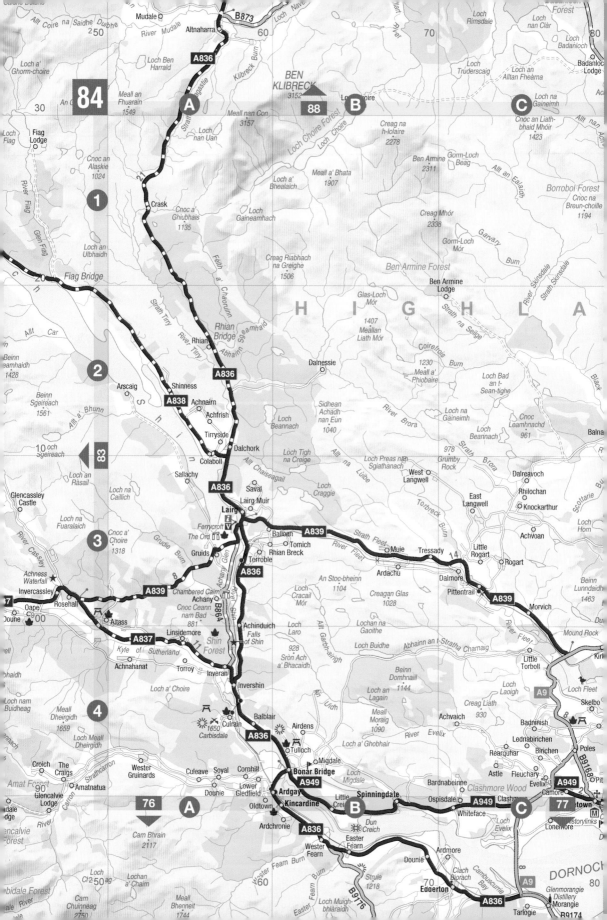

90
²00
10
20

A
B
C

70

1

60

Sheigra
Balchrick
Droman
Oldsho
Beg

Eilean an
Ròin Mór

Kinlo

2

Bàgh Loch
an Ròin

Loch Dughaill

⁹50

Ardmore
Point

Fanagmore

Foindle
Tarbet

Handa
Island

Loch a'
Bhadaidh
Dàraich

Sound of Handa

Scourie Bay

Scourie
More

Scourie

A894

3

Rubh' Aird an
t-Sionnaich

Upper
Badcall

Lower
Badcall

Loch a'
Mhuilinn

40

Badcall Bay

Eilean
a Bhreitheimh

Meall Mór

Duartmore Bridge

Calbha
Beag

Calbha
Mór

Sgeir
nan Gall

Eddrachillis Bay

Loch a' Cha

Point of
Stoer

Oldany
Island

Old Man
of Stoer

Culkein
Drumbeg

Loch
Nedd

B869

4

Loch Cúl
Fraioch

Culkein

Eilean
Chrona

Oldany

Cluas Deas

Rhubha
Stoer

Achnacarnin

Clashnessie
Bay

Drumbeg

Nedd

Glenleraig

16

Loch an
Leothaid

Clashmore

Balchladich

Clashnessie

B869

Loch
Poll

Gorm
Loch Mór

30

A
B
C

Stoer

Loch nan
Lub

Loch na
Loinne

Loch
Beannach

Lochassynt
Lodge

82

Bay of Stoer

Clachtoll
Broch

Clachtoll

Loch
Cròchach

A837

90
²00

Achmelvich Bay

Rhicarn

10

Leireag

Gleann

River Tiaghaich

Alt an

20

Achmelvich

B869

10

Brackloch

Rubha Rodha

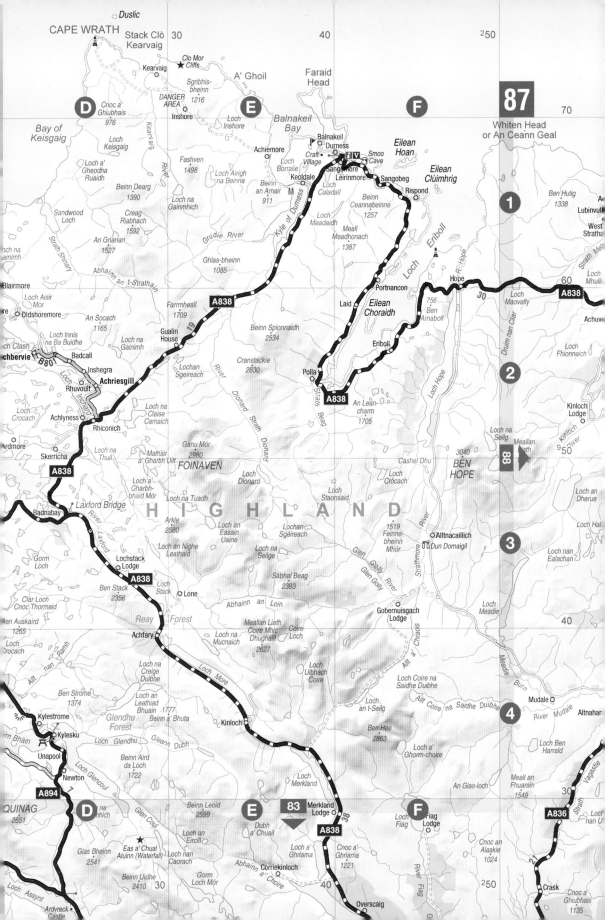

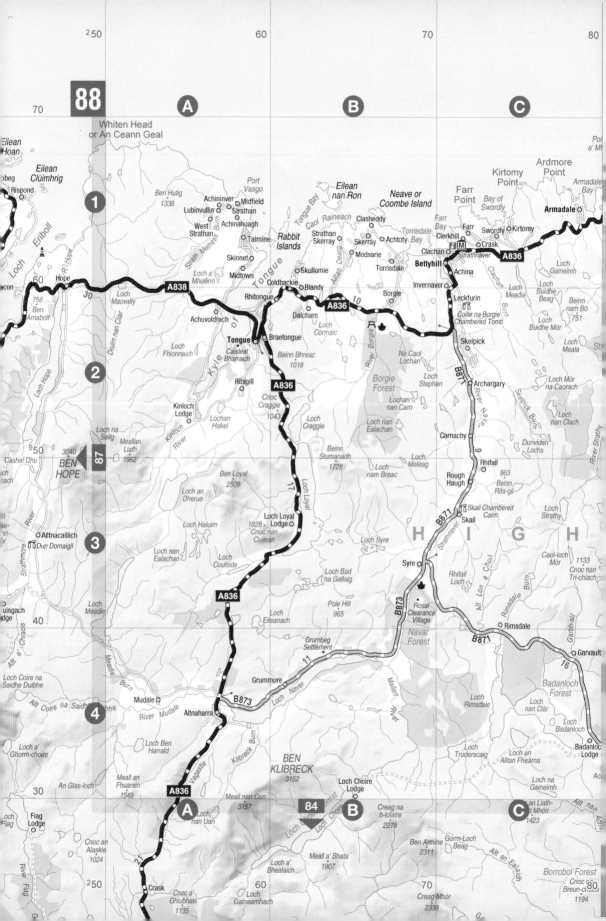

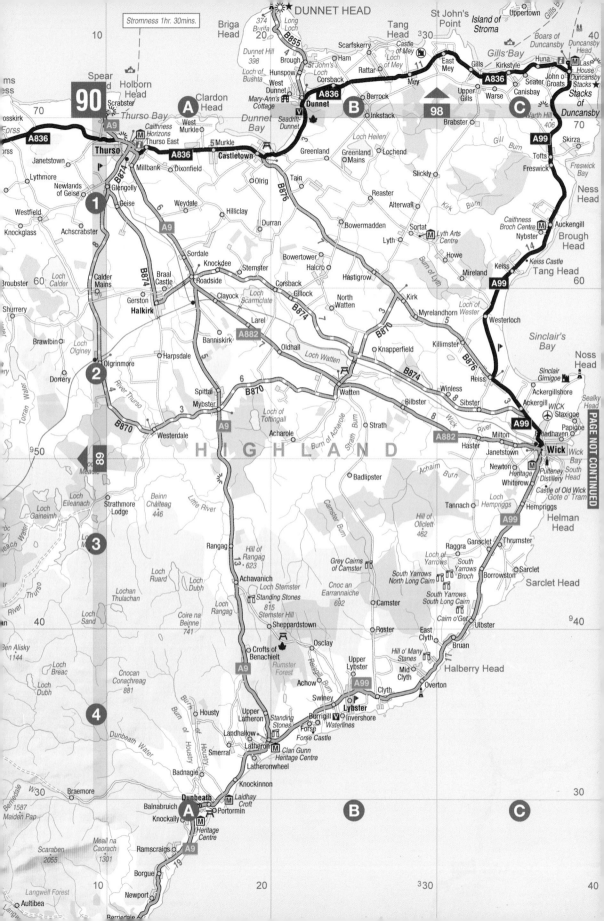

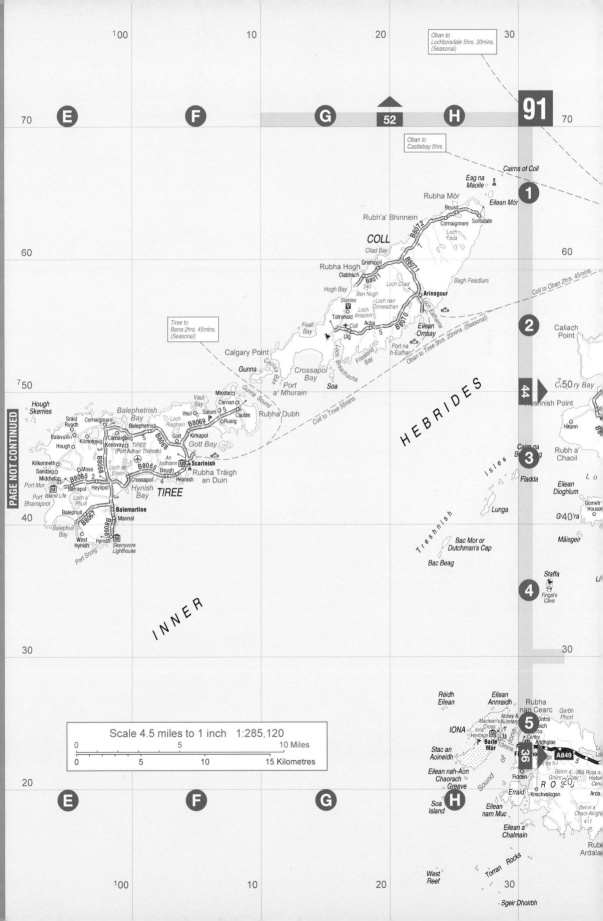

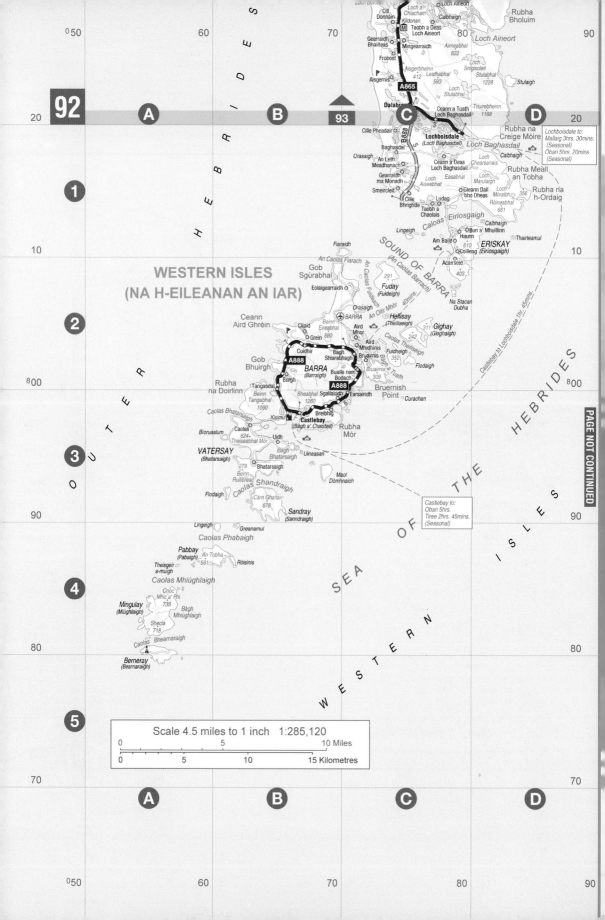

A  B  93  C  D

WESTERN ISLES
(NA H-EILEANAN AN IAR)

Loch Dòmhain
Cill Donnain
Cill Chlachain
Kildonan
Calbhaigh
Taobh a Deas
Loch Aineort
M
Loch Aineort
Gearraidh
Bhailteas
Mingearraidh
Airneabhal 822
Frobost
Aisgernis
Aisgerbheinn 412
Leathabhal 593
Loch Snigiscleit
Stulabhal 1228
Stulaigh
A865
Dalabrog
Loch Stulabhal
Triuirebheinn 1168
Rubha na Creige Móire
Ceann a Tuath Loch Baghasdail
Cille Pheadair
Lochboisdale (Loch Baghasdail)
Loch Baghasdail
Calbhaigh

Lochboisdale to:
Mallaig 3hrs. 30mins.
(Seasonal)
Oban 5hrs. 20mins.
(Seasonal)

Baghasdail
B888
Orasaigh
An Leth Meadhanach
Ceann a Deas Loch Baghasdail
Loch Chearsanais
Rubha Meall an Tobha
Gearraidh na Monadh
Loch Easabhal
Loch Marulaigh
Rubha na h-Ordaig
Smearcleit
Cille Bhrighde
Ludag
Gleann Dail bho Dheas
Loch Mòraibh
Róineabhal 661
356
Taobh a Chaolais
Caolas Eiriosgaigh
Calbhaigh
Lingeigh
Bun a' Mhuillinn
Haunn
Thairteamul
Fiaraidh
Am Baile
610
ERISKAY (Eiriosgaigh)
Coilleag
An Caolas Fiarach
Gob Sgùrabhal
SOUND OF BARRA
(An Caolas Barrach)
Acairseid
403
An Caolas Fuadaigh
291
Fuday (Fuideigh)
Ceann Aird Ghrèin
Cliaid
Beinn Eireabhal 680
BARRA
Orasaigh
An Oitir Mhòr
40mins.
Na Stacan Dubha
Grein
Aird Mhòr
Hellisay (Theileiseigh)
Eolaigearraidh
Gighay (Gioghaigh)
311
Cuidhir
Aird Mhidhinis
Caolas Theiliseigh
242
Gob Bhuirgh
A888
Bàgh Shiarabhagh
Bruairnis
Fuidheigh
Flodaigh
BARRA (Barraigh)
Bualle nam Bodach
Bàgh a Tuath
Rubha na Doirlinn
Tangasdal
Borgh
A888
Bruairnis 309
Sgallairidh
Earsairidh
Bruernish Point
Beinn Tangabhal 1090
Sheabhal 1260
Curachan
Caolas Bhatarsaigh
Kismul
Breibhig
Rubha Mór
Bioruaslum
Caolas
624
Uidh
Castlebay (Bàgh a' Chaisteil)
VATERSAY (Bhatarsaigh)
Theiseabhal Mór
Bàgh Bhatarsaigh
Uineasan
279
Bhatarsaigh
Beinn Ruilibreac
Maol Dòmhnaich

Castlebay to:
Oban 5hrs.
Tiree 2hrs. 45mins.
(Seasonal)

Flodaigh
Caolas Shandraigh
Càrn Ghaltair 678
Sandray (Sanndraigh)
Lingeigh
Greanamul
Caolas Phabaigh
Pabbay (Pabaigh)
An Tobha
561
Ròisinis
Theisgeir a-muigh
Caolas Mhiùghlaigh
Cnòc Mhic a' Phi 735
Bàgh Mhiùghlaigh
Mingulay (Miùghlaigh)
Shecla 718
Bhearnaraigh
Caolas
Berneray (Bearnaraigh)

H E B R I D E S

O U T E R

SEA OF THE HEBRIDES

WESTERN ISLES

PAGE NOT CONTINUED

Castlebay to Lochboisdale 1hr. 45mins.

Scale 4.5 miles to 1 inch   1:285,120

0        5        10 Miles

0      5       10     15 Kilometres

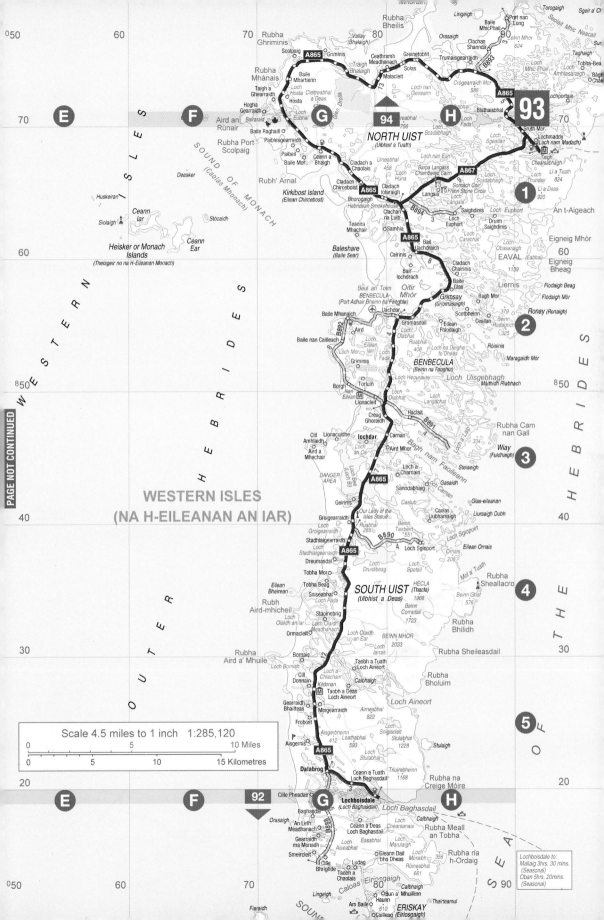

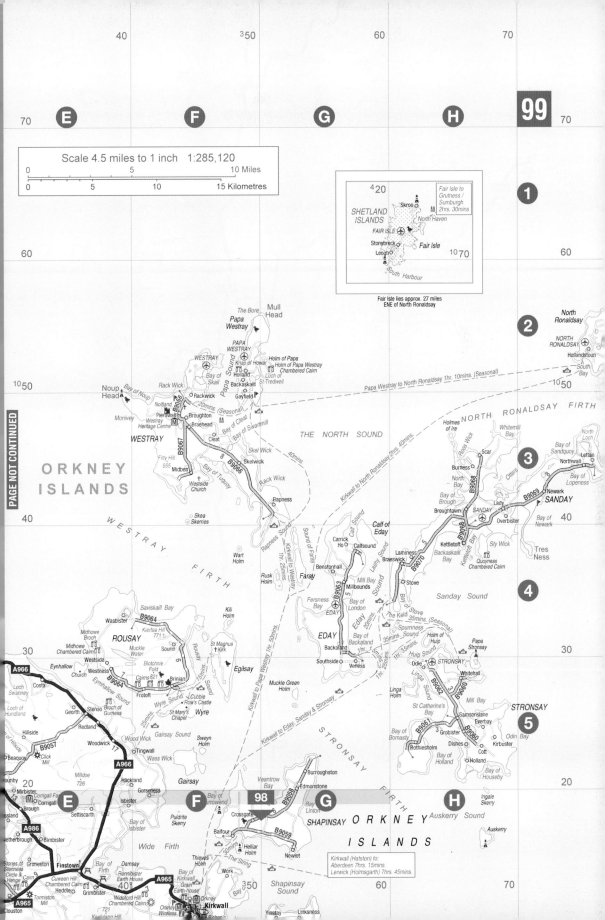

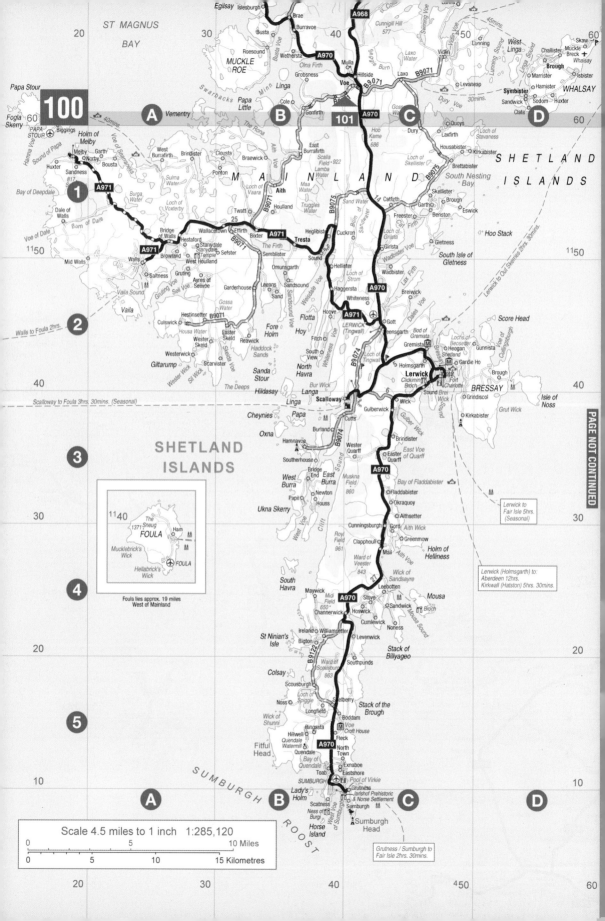

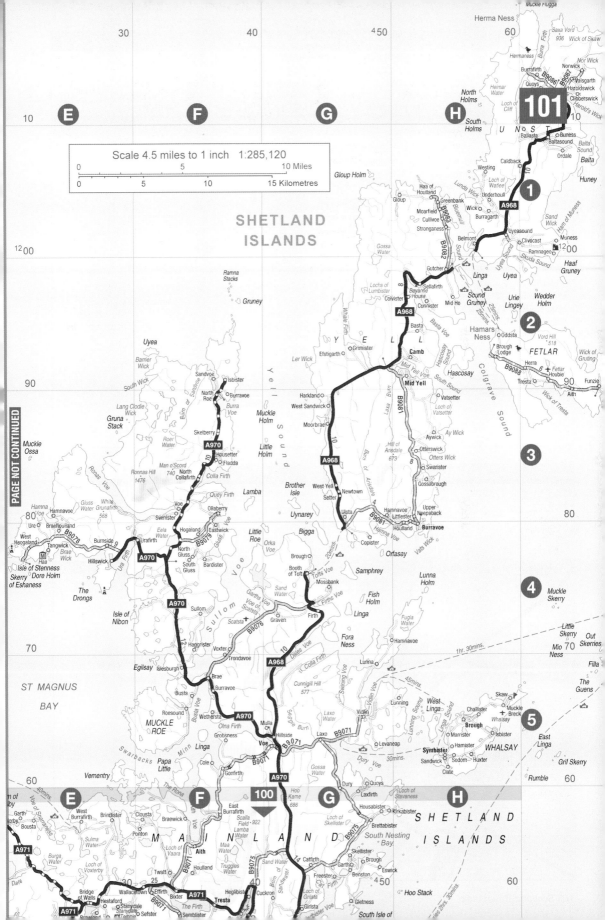

# CITY & TOWN PLANS

## Reference to Town Plans

| | |
|---|---|
| MOTORWAY | **M8** |
| MOTORWAY UNDER CONSTRUCTION | |
| MOTORWAY JUNCTIONS WITH NUMBERS | 4 5 |
| Unlimited Interchange 4  Limited Interchange 5 | |
| PRIMARY ROUTE | A82 |
| DUAL CARRIAGEWAYS | |
| CLASS A ROAD | A910 |
| CLASS B ROAD | B754 |
| MAJOR ROADS UNDER CONSTRUCTION | |
| MAJOR ROADS PROPOSED | |
| MINOR ROADS | |
| RESTRICTED ACCESS | |
| PEDESTRIANIZED ROAD & MAIN FOOTWAY | |
| ONE-WAY STREETS | |
| TOLL | TOLL |
| RAILWAY AND STATION | |
| SUBWAY | |
| LEVEL CROSSING AND TUNNEL | |
| TRAM STOP AND ONE-WAY TRAM STOP | |
| BUILT-UP AREA | |
| ABBEY, CATHEDRAL, PRIORY ETC. | † |

| | |
|---|---|
| BUS STATION | |
| CAR PARK (selection of) | P |
| CHURCH | † |
| CITY WALL | |
| FERRY (Vehicular) | |
| (Foot only) | |
| GOLF COURSE | |
| HELIPORT | |
| HOSPITAL | H |
| LIGHTHOUSE | |
| MARKET | |
| NATIONAL TRUST FOR SCOTLAND PROPERTY (Open) | NTS |
| (Restricted opening) | NTS |
| PARK & RIDE | P+ |
| PLACE OF INTEREST | |
| POLICE STATION | ▲ |
| POST OFFICE | ★ |
| SHOPPING AREA (Main street and precinct) | |
| SHOPMOBILITY | |
| TOILET | |
| TOURIST INFORMATION CENTRE | i |
| VIEWPOINT | |
| VISITOR INFORMATION CENTRE | V |

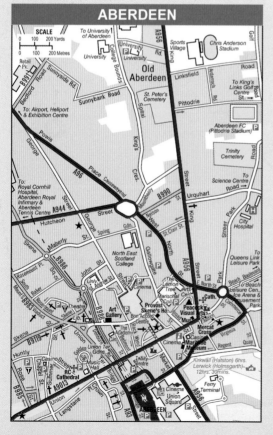

## ABERDEEN

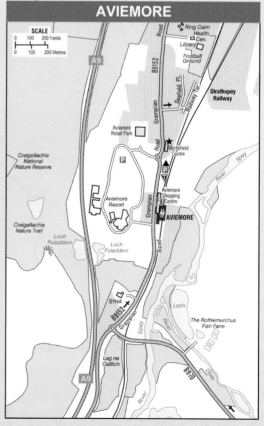

## AVIEMORE

# AYR

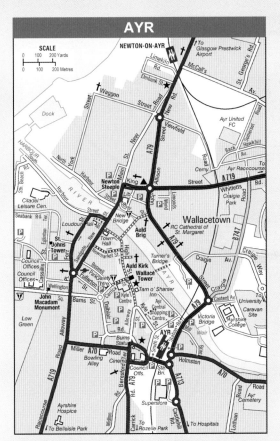

# DUMFRIES

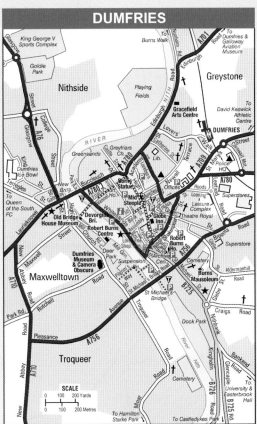

# DUNDEE

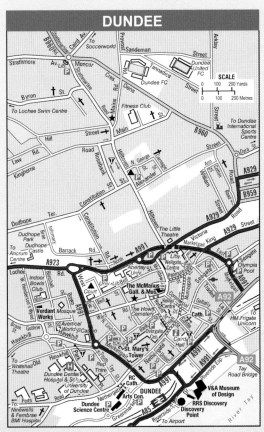

# DUNFERMLINE

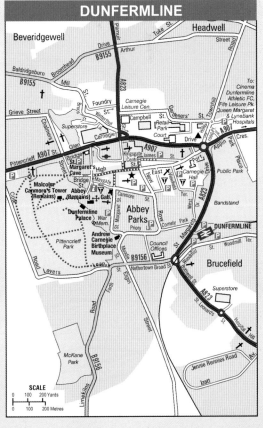

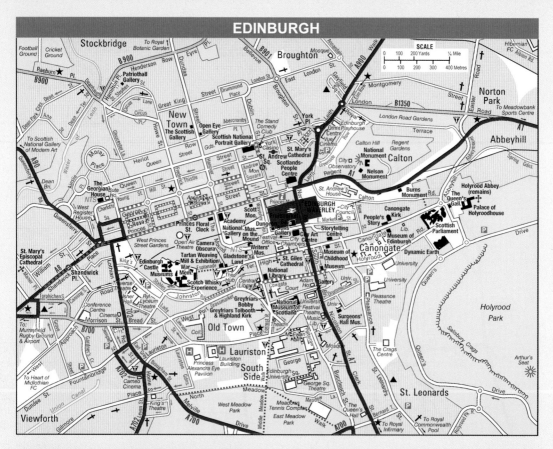

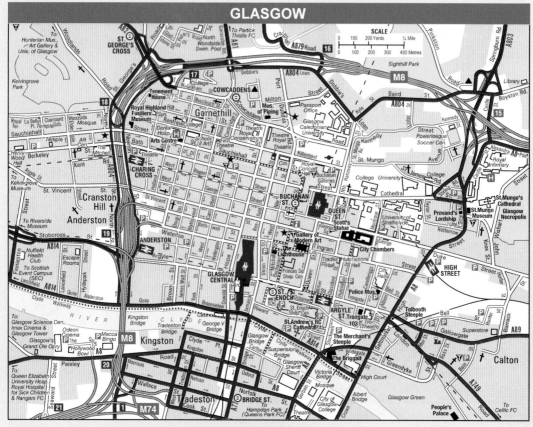

# FALKIRK

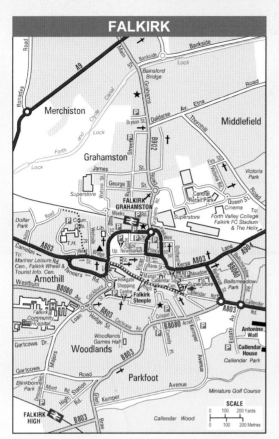

# FORT WILLIAM

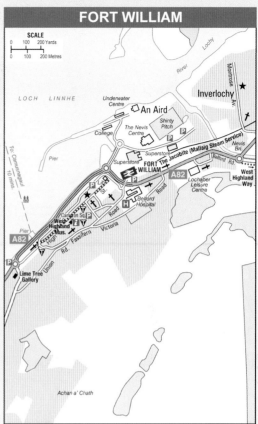

# HAMILTON

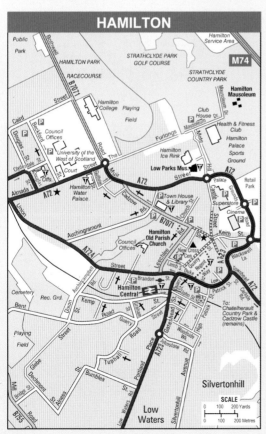

# INVERNESS

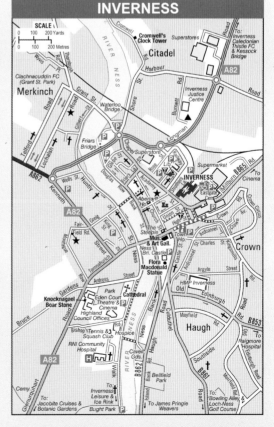

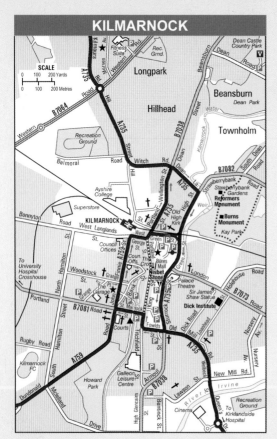

# KILMARNOCK

SCALE
0 100 200 Yards
0 100 200 Metres

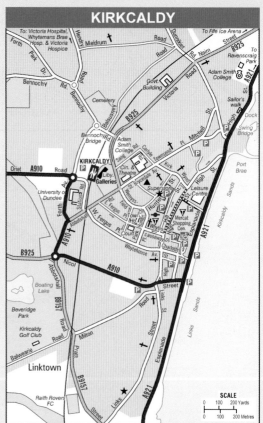

# KIRKCALDY

SCALE
0 100 200 Yards
0 100 200 Metres

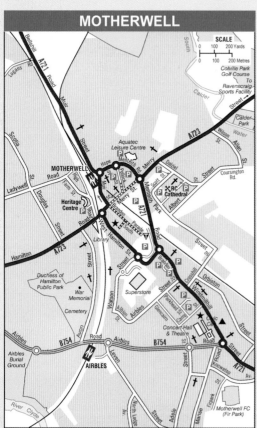

# MOTHERWELL

SCALE
0 100 200 Yards
0 100 200 Metres

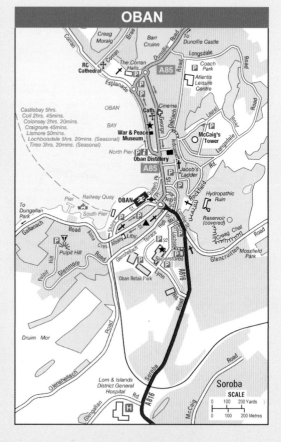

# OBAN

SCALE
0 100 200 Yards
0 100 200 Metres

# PAISLEY

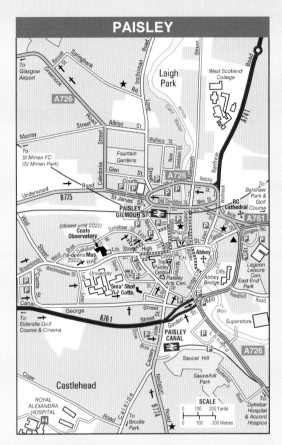

# PERTH

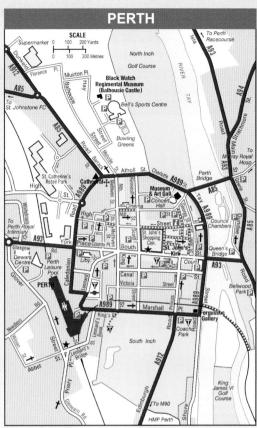

# ST ANDREWS

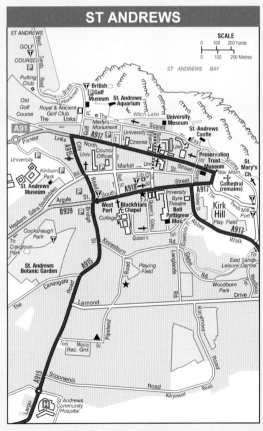

# STIRLING

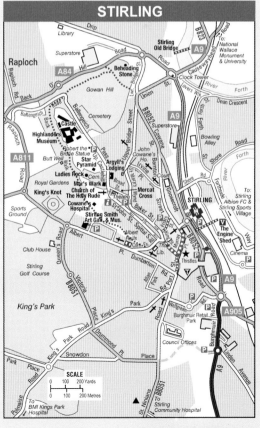

# INDEX TO CITIES, TOWNS, VILLAGES, HAMLETS & LOCATIONS

(1) A strict alphabetical order is used e.g. An Gleann Ur follows Angerton but precedes Ankerville.

(2) The map reference given refers to the actual map square in which the town spot or built-up area is located and not to the place name.

(3) Only one reference is given although due to page overlaps the place may appear on more than one page.

(4) Where two places of the same name occur in the same County or Unitary Authority, the nearest large town is also given;
e.g. Achiemore. *High* . . . .1E **87** (nr. Durness) indicates that Achiemore is located in square 1E on page **87** and is situated near Durness in the Unitary Authority of Highland.

(5) Major towns and destinations are shown in bold i.e. **Aberdeen.** *Aber*. . . .**102** (1E **61**). Page references for Town Plan entries are shown first.

## COUNTIES AND UNITARY AUTHORITIES with the abbreviations used in this index

Aberdeen : *Aber*
Aberdeenshire : *Abers*
Angus : *Ang*
Argyll & Bute : *Arg*
Clackmannanshire : *Clac*
Cumbria : *Cumb*
Dumfries & Galloway : *Dum*
Dundee : *D'dee*
East Ayrshire : *E Ayr*
East Dunbartonshire : *E Dun*
East Lothian : *E Lot*
East Renfrewshire : *E Ren*
Edinburgh : *Edin*
Falkirk : *Falk*
Fife : *Fife*
Glasgow : *Glas*
Highland : *High*
Inverclyde : *Inv*
Midlothian : *Midl*
Moray : *Mor*
North Ayrshire : *N Ayr*
North Lanarkshire : *N Lan*
Northumberland : *Nmbd*
Orkney : *Orkn*
Perth & Kinross : *Per*
Renfrewshire : *Ren*
Scottish Borders : *Bord*
Shetland : *Shet*
South Ayrshire : *S Ayr*
South Lanarkshire : *S Lan*
Stirling : *Stir*
West Dunbartonshire : *W Dun*
Western Isles : *W Isl*
West Lothian : *W Lot*

## A


Abberwick. *Nmbd* 4E **25**
Abbey St Bathans. *Bord* 3D **35**
Abbeytown. *Cumb* 2A **8**
Aberarder. *High* 3D **67**
Aberargie. *Per* 2A **42**
Aberchalder. *High* 1A **56**
Aberchirder. *Abers* 4B **80**
Abercorn. *W Lot* 2C **32**
Abercrombie. *Fife* 3E **43**
Aberdalgie. *Per* 1F **41**
**Aberdeen**. *Aber* **102** (1E **61**)
Aberdeen International Airport. *Aber* 4D **71**
Aberdour. *Fife* 1D **33**
Aberfeldy. *Per* 3D **49**
Aberfoyle. *Stir* 3A **40**
Aberlady. *E Lot* 1A **34**
Aberlemno. *Ang* 2E **51**
Abernethy. *Per* 2A **42**
Abernyte. *Per* 4B **50**
Aberuthven. *Per* 2E **41**
Abhainn Suidhe. *W Isl* 2E **95**
Abington. *S Lan* 3E **21**
Aboyne. *Abers* 2A **60**
Abriachan. *High* 2C **66**
Abronhill. *N Lan* 2F **31**
Abune-the-Hill. *Orkn* 1A **98**
Acairseid. *W Isl* 2C **92**
Acha. *Arg* 2G **91**
Achachork. *High* 1D **63**
Achadh a' Chuirn. *High* 3F **63**
Achahoish. *Arg* 2B **28**
Achaleven. *Arg* 4A **46**
Achallader. *Arg* 3E **47**
Acha Mor. *W Isl* 4E **97**
Achanalt. *High* 3F **75**
Achandunie. *High* 2D **77**
Ach' an Todhair. *High* 4D **55**
Achany. *High* 3A **84**
Achaphubuil. *High* 4D **55**
Acharacle. *High* 1D **45**
Acharn. *Ang* 4D **59**
Acharn. *Per* 3C **48**
Acharole. *High* 2B **90**
Achateny. *High* 1C **44**
Achavanich. *High* 3A **90**
Achdalieu. *High* 4D **55**
Achduart. *High* 3B **82**
Achentoul. *High* 4D **89**
Achfary. *High* 4D **87**
Achfrish. *High* 2A **84**
Achgarve. *High* 1B **74**
Achiemore. *High* 1E **87** (nr. Durness)
Achiemore. *High* 2D **89** (nr. Thurso)
A' Chill. *High* 1B **52**
Achiltibuie. *High* 3B **82**
Achina. *High* 1C **88**
Achinahuagh. *High* 1A **88**
Achindarroch. *High* 2B **46**
Achinduich. *High* 3A **84**
Achinduin. *Arg* 4F **45**
Achininver. *High* 1A **88**
Achintee. *High* 1C **64**
Achintraid. *High* 2B **64**
Achleck. *Arg* 3B **44**
Achlorachan. *High* 4A **76**
Achluachrach. *High* 3F **55**
Achlyness. *High* 2D **87**
Achmelvich. *High* 1B **82**
Achmony. *High* 2C **66**
Achmore. *High* 2B **64** (nr. Stromeferry)
Achmore. *High* 4B **82** (nr. Ullapool)
Achnacarnin. *High* 4B **86**
Achnacarry. *High* 3E **55**
Achnaclerach. *High* 3B **76**
Achnacloich. *High* 1E **53**
Ach na Cloiche. *High* 1E **53**
Achnaconeran. *High* 4B **66**
Achnacroish. *Arg* 3F **45**
Achnafalnich. *Arg* 1D **39**
Achnagarron. *High* 2D **77**
Achnagoul. *Arg* 3B **38**
Achnaha. *High* 1B **44**
Achnahanat. *High* 4A **84**
Achnahannet. *High* 3A **68**
Achnairn. *High* 2A **84**
Achnamara. *Arg* 1B **28**
Achnanellan. *High* 3D **55**
Achnasheen. *High* 4E **75**
Achnashellach. *High* 1D **65**
Achosnich. *High* 1B **44**
Achow. *High* 4B **90**
Achranich. *High* 3E **45**
Achreamie. *High* 1F **89**
Achriabhach. *High* 1C **46**
Achriesgill. *High* 2D **87**
Achrimsdale. *High* 3E **85**
Achscrabster. *High* 1F **89**
Achtoty. *High* 1B **88**
Achuvoldrach. *High* 2A **88**
Achvaich. *High* 4C **84**
Achvoan. *High* 3C **84**
Ackergill. *High* 2C **90**
Ackergillshore. *High* 2C **90**
Adabroc. *W Isl* 1G **97**
Adderstone. *Nmbd* 2E **25**
Addiewell. *W Lot* 3B **32**
Addinston. *Bord* 4B **34**
Advie. *High* 2C **68**
Adziel. *Abers* 4E **81**
Ae. *Dum* 3E **13**
Affleck. *Abers* 3D **71**
Affric Lodge. *High* 3E **65**
Aglionby. *Cumb* 2D **9**
Aiginis. *W Isl* 3F **97**
Aikers. *Orkn* 3C **98**
Aiketgate. *Cumb* 3D **9**
Aikhead. *Cumb* 3B **8**
Aikton. *Cumb* 2B **8**
Ainstable. *Cumb* 3E **9**
Aird. *Arg* 3E **37**
Aird. *Dum* 1B **4**
Aird. *High* 2A **74** (nr. Port Henderson)
Aird. *High* 1E **53** (nr. Tarskavaig)
Aird. *W Isl* 2G **93** (on Benbecula)
Aird. *W Isl* 3G **97** (on Isle of Lewis)
Aird, The. *High* 4D **73**
Àird a Bhasair. *High* 1F **53**
Aird a Mhachair. *W Isl* 3G **93**
Aird a Mhulaidh. *W Isl* 1F **95**
Aird Asaig. *W Isl* 2F **95**
Aird Dhail. *W Isl* 1F **97**
Airdens. *High* 4B **84**
Airdeny. *Arg* 1A **38**
Aird Mhidhinis. *W Isl* 2C **92**
Aird Mhighe. *W Isl* 3F **95** (nr. Ceann a Bhaigh)
Aird Mhighe. *W Isl* 4E **95** (nr. Fionnsabhagh)
Aird Mhor. *W Isl* 2C **92** (on Barra)
Aird Mhor. *W Isl* 3H **93** (on South Uist)
**Airdrie**. *N Lan* 3F **31**
Aird Shleibhe. *W Isl* 4F **95**
Aird Thunga. *W Isl* 3F **97**
Aird Uig. *W Isl* 3B **96**
Airidh a Bhruaich. *W Isl* 1G **95**
Airies. *Dum* 1A **4**
Airntully. *Per* 4F **49**
Airor. *High* 1A **54**
Airth. *Falk* 1B **32**
Aisgernis. *W Isl* 5G **93**
Aith. *Shet* 3H **101** (on Fetlar)
Aith. *Shet* 1B **100** (on Mainland)
Aithsetter. *Shet* 3C **100**
Akeld. *Nmbd* 3C **24**
Albyfield. *Cumb* 2E **9**
Alcaig. *High* 4C **76**
Aldclune. *Per* 1E **49**
Aldochlay. *Arg* 4E **39**
Aldoth. *Cumb* 3A **8**
Alexandria. *W Dun* 1B **30**
Alford. *Abers* 4A **70**
Aline Lodge. *W Isl* 1F **95**
Alladale Lodge. *High* 1B **76**
Allanbank. *N Lan* 4A **32**
Allanton. *N Lan* 4A **32**
Allanton. *Bord* 4E **35**
Allerby. *Cumb* 4F **7**
Alligin Shuas. *High* 4B **74**
**Alloa**. *Clac* 4D **41**
Allonby. *Cumb* 3F **7**
Alloway. *S Ayr* 4E **19**
Alltgobhlach. *N Ayr* 1F **17**
Alltnacaillich. *High* 3F **87**
Allt na h' Airbhe. *High* 4C **82**
Alltour. *High* 3F **55**
Alltsigh. *High* 4B **66**
Almondbank. *Per* 1F **41**
Alness. *High* 3D **77**
Alnessferry. *High* 3D **77**
Alnham. *Nmbd* 4C **24**
Alnmouth. *Nmbd* 4F **25**
**Alnwick**. *Nmbd* 4E **25**
Alston. *Cumb* 3F **9**
Altandhu. *High* 2A **82**
Altanduin. *High* 1D **85**
Altass. *High* 3F **83**
Alterwall. *High* 1B **90**
Altgaltraig. *Arg* 2E **29**
Altnabreac. *High* 3F **89**
Altnacealgach. *High* 2D **83**
Altnafeadh. *High* 2D **47**
Altnaharra. *High* 4A **88**
Altonhill. *E Ayr* 2F **19**
Altrua. *High* 2F **55**
Alva. *Clac* 4D **41**
Alves. *Mor* 3C **78**
Alvie. *High* 1F **57**
Alwinton. *Nmbd* 4C **24**
Alyth. *Per* 3B **50**
Amatnatua. *High* 4F **83**
Am Baile. *W Isl* 1C **92**
Amble. *Nmbd* 4F **25**
Amisfield. *Dum* 3F **13**
Amulree. *Per* 4E **49**
Anaheilt. *High* 1F **45**
An Àird. *High* 1E **53**
An Camus Darach. *High* 2F **53**
An Cnoc. *W Isl* 3F **97**
An Cnoc Ard. *W Isl* 1G **97**
An Coroghon. *High* 1B **52**
Ancroft. *Nmbd* 1D **25**
Ancrum. *Bord* 3F **23**
An Dùnan. *High* 3E **63**
Angerton. *Cumb* 2B **8**
An Gleann Ur. *W Isl* 3F **97**
Ankerville. *High* 2F **77**
An Leth Meadhanach. *W Isl* 1C **92**
Annan. *Dum* 1B **8**
Annat. *Arg* 1B **38**
Annat. *High* 4B **74**
Annathill. *N Lan* 2F **31**
Annbank. *S Ayr* 3F **19**
An Sailean. *High* 1D **45**
Anston. *S Lan* 1F **21**
Anstruther Easter. *Fife* 3E **43**
Anstruther Wester. *Fife* 3E **43**
An Taobh Tuath. *W Isl* 4D **94**
An t-Aodann Ban. *High* 4C **72**
An t Ath Leathann. *High* 3F **63**
An Teanga. *High* 1F **53**
Anthorn. *Cumb* 2A **8**
An t-Ob. *W Isl* 4E **95**
An t-Òrd. *High* 4F **63**
Anwoth. *Dum* 2A **6**
Appin. *Arg* 3A **46**
Applecross. *High* 1A **64**
Applegarthtown. *Dum* 3A **14**
Applethwaite. *Cumb* 4B **8**
Appletreehall. *Bord* 4E **23**
Arabella. *High* 2F **77**
Arasaig. *High* 3F **53**
Arbeadie. *Abers* 2B **60**
Arbirlot. *Ang* 3F **51**
**Arbroath**. *Ang* 3F **51**
Arbuthnott. *Abers* 4D **61**
Arcan. *High* 4C **76**
Archargary. *High* 2C **88**
Archiestown. *Mor* 1D **69**
Ardachu. *High* 3B **84**
Ardalanish. *Arg* 2A **36**
Ardaneaskan. *High* 2B **64**
Ardarroch. *High* 2B **64**
Ardbeg. *Arg* 1F **29** (nr. Dunoon)
Ardbeg. *Arg* 1B **16** (on Islay)
Ardbeg. *Arg* 3E **29** (on Isle of Bute)
Ardcharnich. *High* 1E **75**
Ardchiavaig. *Arg* 2A **36**
Ardchonnell. *Arg* 2A **38**
Ardchrishnish. *Arg* 1B **36**
Ardchronie. *High* 1D **77**
Ardchullarie. *Stir* 2A **40**
Ardchyle. *Stir* 1A **40**
Ard-dhubh. *High* 1A **64**
Ardechive. *High* 2E **55**
Ardelve. *High* 3B **64**
Arden. *Arg* 1B **30**
Ardendrain. *High* 2C **66**
Ardentinny. *Arg* 1F **29**
Ardeonaig. *Stir* 4B **48**
Ardersier. *High* 4E **77**
Ardery. *High* 1E **45**
Ardessie. *High* 1D **75**
Ardfern. *Arg* 3F **37**
Ardfernal. *Arg* 2F **27**
Ardfin. *Arg* 3E **27**
Ardgartan. *Arg* 3D **39**
Ardgay. *High* 4B **84**
Ardgour. *High* 1B **46**
Ardheslaig. *High* 4A **74**
Ardindrean. *High* 1E **75**
Ardlamont House. *Arg* 3D **29**
Ardler. *Per* 3B **50**
Ardlui. *Arg* 2E **39**
Ardlussa. *Arg* 1A **28**
Ardmair. *High* 4C **82**
Ardmay. *Arg* 3D **39**
Ardminish. *Arg* 1D **17**
Ardmolich. *High* 4A **54**
Ardmore. *High* 2D **87** (nr. Kinlochbervie)
Ardmore. *High* 1E **77** (nr. Tain)
Ardnacross. *Arg* 3C **44**
Ardnadam. *Arg* 1F **29**
Ardnagrask. *High* 1C **66**
Ardnamurach. *High* 2B **54**
Ardnarff. *High* 2B **64**
Ardnastang. *High* 1F **45**
Ardoch. *Per* 4F **49**
Ardochy House. *High* 1F **55**
Ardpatrick. *Arg* 3B **28**
Ardrishaig. *Arg* 1C **28**
Ardroag. *High* 1B **62**
Ardross. *High* 2D **77**
**Ardrossan**. *N Ayr* 1D **19**
Ardshealach. *High* 1E **45**
Ardslignish. *High* 1C **44**
Ardtalla. *Arg* 4E **27**
Ardtalnaig. *Per* 4C **48**
Ardtoe. *High* 4F **53**
Arduaine. *Arg* 2E **37**
Ardullie. *High* 3C **76**
Ardvasar. *High* 1F **53**
Ardvorlich. *Per* 1B **40**
Ardwell. *Dum* 3C **4**
Ardwell. *Mor* 2E **69**
Arean. *High* 4F **53**
Aridhglas. *Arg* 1A **36**
Arinacrinachd. *High* 4A **74**
Arinagour. *Arg* 2H **91**
Arisaig. *High* 3F **53**
Ariundle. *High* 1F **45**
Arivegaig. *High* 1D **45**
Armadail. *High* 1F **53**
Armadale. *High* 1F **53** (nr. Isleornsay)
Armadale. *High* 1C **88** (nr. Strathy)
Armadale. *W Lot* 3B **32**
Armathwaite. *Cumb* 3E **9**
Arncroach. *Fife* 3E **43**
Arnicle. *Arg* 2E **17**
Arnisdale. *High* 4B **64**
Arnish. *High* 1E **63**
Arniston. *Midl* 3F **33**
Arnol. *W Isl* 2E **97**
Arnprior. *Stir* 4B **40**
Aros Mains. *Arg* 3C **44**
Arpafeelie. *High* 4D **77**
Arrochar. *Arg* 3D **39**
Arscaig. *High* 2A **84**
Artafallie. *High* 1D **67**
Arthrath. *Abers* 2E **71**
Arthurstone. *Per* 3B **50**
Ascog. *Arg* 3F **29**
Ashfield. *Stir* 3C **40**
Ashgill. *S Lan* 1C **20**
Ashgrove. *Mor* 3D **79**
Ashkirk. *Bord* 3D **23**
Ashton. *Inv* 2A **30**
Askham. *Cumb* 4E **9**
Aspatria. *Cumb* 3A **8**
Astle. *High* 4C **84**
Athelstaneford. *E Lot* 2B **34**
Ath-Tharracail. *High* 1D **45**
Attadale. *High* 2C **64**
Aucharnie. *Abers* 1B **70**
Auchattie. *Abers* 2B **60**
Auchavan. *Ang* 1A **50**
Auchbreck. *Mor* 3D **69**
Auchenback. *E Ren* 4D **31**
Auchenblae. *Abers* 4C **60**
Auchenbrack. *Dum* 2C **12**
Auchenbreck. *Arg* 1E **29**
Auchencairn. *Dum* 2C **6** (nr. Dalbeattie)
Auchencairn. *Dum* 3E **13** (nr. Dumfries)
Auchencarroch. *W Dun* 1C **30**
Auchencrow. *Bord* 3E **35**
Auchendennan. *Arg* 1B **30**
Auchendinny. *Midl* 3E **33**
Auchengray. *S Lan* 4B **32**
Auchenhalrig. *Mor* 3E **79**
Auchenheath. *S Lan* 1D **21**
Auchenlochan. *Arg* 2D **29**
Auchenmade. *N Ayr* 1E **19**
Auchenmalg. *Dum* 2D **5**
Auchentiber. *N Ayr* 1E **19**
Auchenvennel. *Arg* 1A **30**
Auchindrain. *Arg* 3B **38**
Auchininna. *Abers* 1B **70**
Auchinleck. *Dum* 4F **11**
Auchinleck. *E Ayr* 3A **20**
Auchinloch. *N Lan* 2E **31**
Auchinstarry. *N Lan* 2F **31**
Auchleven. *Abers* 3B **70**
Auchlochan. *S Lan* 2D **21**
Auchlunachan. *High* 1E **75**
Auchmillan. *E Ayr* 3A **20**
Auchmithie. *Ang* 3F **51**
Auchmuirbridge. *Fife* 3B **42**
Auchmull. *Ang* 4A **60**
Auchnacree. *Ang* 1D **51**
Auchnafree. *Per* 4D **49**
Auchnagallin. *High* 2B **68**
Auchnagatt. *Abers* 1E **71**
Aucholzie. *Abers* 2E **59**
Auchreddie. *Abers* 1D **71**
Auchterarder. *Per* 2E **41**
Auchteraw. *High* 1A **56**
Auchterderran. *Fife* 4B **42**
Auchterhouse. *Ang* 4C **50**
Auchtermuchty. *Fife* 2B **42**
Auchterneed. *High* 4B **76**
Auchtertool. *Fife* 4B **42**
Auchtertyre. *High* 3B **64**
Auchtubh. *Stir* 1A **40**
Auckengill. *High* 1C **90**
Auds. *Abers* 3B **80**
Aughertree. *Cumb* 4B **8**
Auldearn. *High* 4A **78**
Auldgirth. *Dum* 3E **13**
Auldhouse. *S Lan* 4E **31**
Ault a' chruinn. *High* 3C **64**
Aultbea. *High* 1B **74**
Aultdearg. *High* 3F **75**
Aultgrishan. *High* 1A **74**
Aultguish Inn. *High* 2A **76**
Aultibea. *High* 1F **85**
Aultiphurst. *High* 1D **89**
Aultivullin. *High* 1D **89**
Aultmore. *Mor* 4F **79**
Aultnamain Inn. *High* 1D **77**
Avielochan. *High* 4A **68**
**Aviemore**. *High* **102** (4F **67**)

Clachan—Dalsmirren


Clachan. Arg 4B 28
(on Kintyre)
Clachan. Arg 3F 45
(on Lismore)
Clachan. High 1C 88
(nr. Bettyhill)
Clachan. High 3D 73
(nr. Staffin)
Clachan. High 2D 73
(nr. Uig)
Clachan. High 2E 63
(on Raasay)
Clachan Farm. Arg 2C 38
Clachan na Luib. W Isl 1H 93
Clachan of Campsie. E Dun 2E 31
Clachan of Glendaruel. Arg 1D 29
Clachan-Seil. Arg 2E 37
Clachan Shannda. W Isl 5C 94
Clachan Strachur. Arg 3B 38
Clachbreck. Arg 2B 28
Clachnaharry. High 1D 67
Clachtoll. High 1B 82
Clackmannan. Clac 4E 41
**Clackmannanshire Bridge**.
Clac 1B 32
Clackmarras. Mor 4D 79
Cladach a Chaolais. W Isl 1G 93
Cladach Chairinis. W Isl 2H 93
Cladach Chirceboist. W Isl 1G 93
Cladach Iolaraigh. W Isl 1G 93
Cladich. Arg 1B 38
Claggan. High 4E 55
(nr. Fort William)
Claggan. High 2E 45
(nr. Lochaline)
Claigan. High 4B 72
Claonaig. Arg 4C 28
Clappers. Bord 4F 35
Clapphoull. Shet 4C 100
Clarebrand. Dum 1C 6
Clarencefield. Dum 1F 7
Clarilaw. Bord 4E 23
**Clarkston**. E Ren 4D 31
Clasheddy. High 1B 88
Clashindarroch. Abers 2F 69
Clashmore. High 1E 77
(nr. Dornoch)
Clashmore. High 4B 86
(nr. Stoer)
Clashnessie. High 4B 86
Clashnoir. Mor 3D 69
Clate. Shet 5H 101
Clathick. Per 1D 41
Clathy. Per 2E 41
Clatt. Abers 3A 70
Claygate. Dum 4C 14
Clayholes. Ang 4E 51
Clayock. High 2A 90
Cleadale. High 3D 53
Cleat. Orkn 3F 99
(nr. Braehead)
Cleat. Orkn 4C 98
(nr. St Margaret's Hope)
Cleekhimin. N Lan 4F 31
Cleigh. Arg 1F 37
Cleish. Per 4F 41
Cleland. N Lan 4A 32
Clennell. Nmbd 4C 24
Clephanton. High 4F 77
Clerkhill. High 1C 88
Clestrain. Orkn 2B 98
Cliaid. W Isl 2B 92
Cliasmol. W Isl 2E 95
Clibberswick. Shet 1H 101
Cliburn. Cumb 4E 9
Cliffburn. Ang 3F 51
Clifton. Cumb 4E 9
Clifton. Stir 4E 47
Climpy. S Lan 4B 32
Clintmains. Bord 2F 23
Cliobh. W Isl 3B 96
Cliuthar. W Isl 3F 95
Clivocast. Shet 1H 101
Clochan. Mor 3F 79
Clochforbie. Abers 4D 81
Cloddymoss. Mor 3A 78
Clola. Abers 1F 71
Closeburn. Dum 2D 13
Clousta. Shet 1B 100
Clouston. Orkn 1A 98
Clova. Abers 3F 69
Clova. Ang 4E 59
Clovenfords. Bord 2D 23
Clovenstone. Abers 4C 70
Clovullin. High 1B 46
Cluanie Inn. High 4D 65
Cluanie Lodge. High 4D 65
Clunas. High 1F 67
Clune. High 3E 67
Clunes. High 3F 55
Clunie. Per 3A 50
Cluny. Fife 4B 42
**Clydebank**. W Dun 3D 31
Clynder. Arg 1A 30
Clynelish. High 3D 85
Clyth. High 4B 90
Cnip. W Isl 3B 96
Cnoc Amhlaigh. W Isl 3G 97
Coalburn. S Lan 2D 21
Coalford. Abers 2D 61
Coalhall. E Ayr 4F 19
Coalsnaughton. Clac 4E 41
Coaltown of Balgonie. Fife 4C 42
Coaltown of Wemyss. Fife 4C 42
Coanwood. Nmbd 2F 9
**Coatbridge**. N Lan 3F 31
Coatdyke. N Lan 3F 31
Cock Bridge. Abers 1D 59
Cockburnspath. Bord 2D 35
Cockenzie and Port Seton.
E Lot 2A 34
Cockermouth. Cumb 4A 8
Cocklaw. Abers 1F 71
Cockmuir. Abers 4E 81
Coignafearn Lodge. High 4D 67
Coig Peighinnean. W Isl 1G 97
Coig Peighinnean Bhuirgh.
W Isl 1F 97
Coilleag. W Isl 1C 92
Coillemore. High 2D 77
Coillore. High 2C 62
Coire an Fhuarain. W Isl 3D 96
Col. W Isl 2F 97
Colaboll. High 2A 84
Colbost. High 1B 62
Coldbackie. High 2B 88
Coldingham. Bord 3F 35
Coldrain. Per 3F 41
Coldstream. Bord 1B 24
Coldwells. Abers 2F 71
Coldwells Croft. Abers 3A 70
Cole. Shet 5F 101
Coleburn. Mor 4D 79
Colinsburgh. Fife 3D 43
Colinton. Edin 3E 33
Colintraive. Arg 2E 29
Collace. Per 4B 50
Collam. W Isl 3F 95
College of Roseisle. Mor 3C 78
Collessie. Fife 2B 42
Collieston. Abers 3F 71
Collin. Dum 4F 13
Colliston. Ang 3F 51
Collydean. Fife 3B 42
Colmonell. S Ayr 3C 10
Colpy. Abers 2B 70
Colstoun House. E Lot 2B 34
Coltfield. Mor 3C 78
Coltness. N Lan 4A 32
Col Uarach. W Isl 3F 97
Colvend. Dum 2D 7
Colvister. Shet 2H 101
Comers. Abers 1B 60
Comrie. Fife 1C 32
Comrie. Per 1C 40
Conaglen. High 1B 46
Conchra. Arg 1E 29
Conchra. High 3B 64
Condorrat. N Lan 2F 31
Conicaval. Mor 4A 78
Conisby. Arg 3C 26
Connel. Arg 4A 46
Connel Park. E Ayr 4B 20
Connista. High 2D 73
Conon Bridge. High 4C 76
Cononsyth. Ang 3E 51
Conordan. High 2E 63
Contin. High 4B 76
Contullich. High 2D 77
Cookney. Abers 2D 61
Copister. Shet 4G 101
Copshaw Holm. Bord 3D 15
Cordon. N Ayr 2B 18
Corgarff. Abers 1D 59
Corlae. Dum 2B 12
Cormiston. S Lan 2F 21
Cornaigbeg. Arg 3E 91
Cornaigmore. Arg 1H 91
(on Coll)
Cornaigmore. Arg 3E 91
(on Tiree)
Cornhill. Abers 4A 80
Cornhill. High 4A 84
Cornhill-on-Tweed. Nmbd 2B 24
Cornquoy. Orkn 2D 98
Corntown. High 4C 76
Corpach. High 4D 55
Corra. Dum 1D 7
Corran. High 1B 46
(nr. Arnisdale)
Corran. High 1B 54
(nr. Fort William)
Corribeg. High 4C 54
Corrie. N Ayr 1B 18
Corrie Common. Dum 3B 14
Corriecravie. N Ayr 3A 18
Corriekinloch. High 1E 83
Corriemoillie. High 3A 76
Corrievarkie Lodge. Per 4C 56
Corrievorrie. High 3E 67
Corrigall. Orkn 1B 98
Corrimony. High 2A 66
Corrour Shooting Lodge.
High 1F 47
Corry. High 3F 63
Corrybrough. High 3F 67
Corrygills. N Ayr 2B 18
Corry of Ardnagrask. High 1C 66
Corsback. High 5A 98
(nr. Dunnet)
Corsback. High 2B 90
(nr. Halkirk)
Corse. Abers 1B 70
Corsehill. Abers 4E 81
Corse of Kinnoir. Abers 1A 70
Corsock. Dum 4C 12
Corstorphine. Edin 2E 33
Cortachy. Ang 2C 50
Corwar House. S Ayr 3D 11
Costa. Orkn 5E 99
Cotehill. Cumb 2D 9
Cothal. Abers 4D 71
Cott. Orkn 5H 99
Cottartown. High 2B 68
Cottown. Abers 1D 71
Coulags. High 1C 64
Coulin Lodge. High 4D 75
Coull. Abers 1A 60
Coulport. Arg 1A 30
Coulter. S Lan 2F 21
Coupar Angus. Per 3B 50
Coupland. Nmbd 2C 24
Cour. Arg 1F 17
Courance. Dum 2F 13
Courteachan. High 2F 53
Cousland. Midl 3F 33
Coustonn. Arg 2E 29
Cove. Arg 1A 30
Cove. High 1B 74
Cove. Bord 2D 35
Cove Bay. Aber 1E 61
Covesea. Mor 2C 78
Covington. S Lan 2E 21
**Cowdenbeath**. Fife 4A 42
Cowdenburn. Bord 4E 33
Cowdenend. Fife 4A 42
Cowfords. Mor 3E 79
Cowie. Abers 3D 61
Cowie. Stir 1A 32
Cowstrandburn. Fife 4F 41
Coylton. S Ayr 4F 19
Coylumbridge. High 4A 68
Coynach. Abers 1F 59
Coynachie. Abers 2F 69
Crackaig. High 2E 85
Cradhlastadh. W Isl 3B 96
Cragabus. Arg 1A 16
Craggan. High 3B 68
Cragganmore. Mor 2C 68
Cragganvallie. High 2C 66
Craggie. High 2D 85
Craggiemore. High 2E 67
Craichie. Ang 3E 51
Craig. Arg 4B 46
Craig. Dum 4B 12
Craig. High 1D 65
(nr. Achnashellach)
Craig. High 3A 74
(nr. Lower Diabaig)
Craig. High 2B 64
(nr. Stromeferry)
Craiganour Lodge. Per 2B 48
Craigbrack. Arg 4C 38
Craigdallie. Per 1B 42
Craigdam. Abers 2D 71
Craigdarroch. E Ayr 1B 12
Craigdarroch. High 4B 76
Craigdhu. High 1B 66
Craigearn. Abers 4C 70
Craigellachie. Mor 1D 69
Craigend. Per 1A 42
Craigendoran. Arg 1B 30
Craigends. Ren 3C 30
Craigenputtock. Dum 3C 12
Craigens. E Ayr 4A 20
Craighall. Edin 2D 33
Craighead. Fife 2F 43
Craighouse. Arg 3F 27
Craigie. Abers 4E 71
Craigie. D'dee 4D 51
Craigie. Per 3A 50
(nr. Blairgowrie)
Craigie. Per 1A 42
(nr. Perth)
Craigie. S Ayr 2F 19
Craigielaw. E Lot 2A 34
Craiglemine. Dum 4F 5
Craiglockhart. Edin 2E 33
Craig Lodge. Arg 2E 29
Craigmalloch. E Ayr 2F 11
Craigmaud. Abers 4D 81
Craigmill. Stir 4D 41
Craigmillar. Edin 2E 33
Craigmore. Arg 3F 29
Craigmuie. Dum 3C 12
Craignair. Dum 1D 7
Craigneuk. N Lan 3F 31
(nr. Airdrie)
Craigneuk. N Lan 4F 31
(nr. Motherwell)
Craignure. Arg 4E 45
Craigo. Ang 1F 51
Craigrory. High 1D 67
Craigrothie. Fife 2C 42
Craigs. Dum 4B 14
Craigs, The. High 4F 83
Craigshill. W Lot 3C 32
Craigton. Aber 1D 61
Craigton. Abers 1C 60
Craigton. Ang 4E 51
(nr. Carnoustie)
Craigton. Ang 2C 50
(nr. Kirriemuir)
Craigton. High 1D 67
Craigtown. High 2D 89
Craik. Bord 1C 14
Crail. Fife 3F 43
Crailing. Bord 3F 23
Crailinghall. Bord 3F 23
Cramond. Edin 2D 33
Cramond Bridge. Edin 2D 33
Cranloch. Mor 4D 79
Crannich. Arg 3C 44
Crannoch. Mor 4F 79
Cranshaws. Bord 3C 34
Craobh Haven. Arg 3E 37
Craobhnaclag. High 1B 66
Crarae. Arg 4A 38
Crask. High 1C 88
(nr. Bettyhill)
Crask. High 1A 84
(nr. Lairg)
Crask of Aigas. High 1B 66
Craster. Nmbd 3F 25
Crathes. Abers 2C 60
Crathie. Abers 2D 59
Crathie. High 2C 56
Crawford. S Lan 3E 21
Crawforddyke. S Lan 4A 32
Crawfordjohn. S Lan 3D 21
Crawick. Dum 4C 20
Crawton. Abers 3D 61
Cray. Per 1A 50
Creagan. Arg 3A 46
Creag Aoil. High 4E 55
Creag Ghoraidh. W Isl 3G 93
Creaguaineach Lodge. High 1E 47
Creca. Dum 4B 14
Creebridge. Dum 1F 5
Creetown. Dum 2F 5
Creggans. Arg 3B 38
Creich. Arg 1A 36
Creich. Fife 1C 42
Crepkill. High 1D 63
**Crianlarich**. Stir 1E 39
Crichton. Midl 3F 33
Crieff. Per 1D 41
Crimond. Abers 4F 81
Crimonmogate. Abers 4F 81
Crinan. Arg 4E 37
Crocketford. Dum 4D 13
Croftamie. Stir 1C 30
Croftfoot. Glas 3D 31
Croftmill. Per 4D 49
Crofton. Cumb 2C 8
Crofts. Dum 4C 12
Crofts of Benachielt. High 4A 90
Crofts of Dipple. Mor 4E 79
Croggan. Arg 1E 37
Croglin. Cumb 3E 9
Croich. High 4F 83
Croick. High 2D 89
Croig. Arg 2A 44
Cromarty. High 3E 77
Crombie. Fife 1C 32
Cromdale. High 3B 68
Cromor. W Isl 4F 97
Cromra. High 3C 56
Cronberry. E Ayr 3B 20
Crookdake. Cumb 3A 8
Crookedholm. E Ayr 2F 19
Crookham. Nmbd 2C 24
Crook of Devon. Per 3F 41
Crookston. Glas 3D 31
Cros. W Isl 1G 97
Crosbie. N Ayr 4A 30
Crosbost. W Isl 4E 97
Crosby. Cumb 4F 7
Crosby Villa. Cumb 4F 7
Crossaig. Arg 4C 28
Crossapol. Arg 3E 91
Crosscanonby. Cumb 4F 7
Crossford. Fife 1C 32
Crossford. S Lan 1D 21
Crossgate. Orkn 1C 98
Crossgatehall. E Lot 3F 33
Crossgates. Fife 1D 33
Crosshands. E Ayr 2F 19
Crosshill. E Ayr 3F 19
Crosshill. Fife 4A 42
Crosshill. S Ayr 1E 11
Crosshills. High 2D 77
Crosshouse. E Ayr 2E 19
Crossings. Cumb 4E 15
Crosskirk. High 1F 89
Crosslee. Ren 3C 30
Crossmichael. Dum 1C 6
Cross of Jackston. Abers 2C 70
Crossroads. Abers 1E 61
(nr. Aberdeen)
Crossroads. Abers 2C 60
(nr. Banchory)
Crossroads. E Ayr 2F 19
Crosston. Ang 2E 51
Crothair. W Isl 3C 96
Crovie. Abers 3D 81
Croy. High 1E 67
Croy. N Lan 2F 31
Crubenbeg. High 2D 57
Crubenmore Lodge. High 2D 57
Cruden Bay. Abers 2F 71
Crudie. Abers 4C 80
Crulabhig. W Isl 3C 96
Cuaich. High 3D 57
Cuaig. High 4A 74
Cuan. Arg 2E 37
Cuckron. Shet 1C 100
Cuidhir. W Isl 2B 92
Cuidhsiadar. W Isl 1G 97
Cuidhtinis. W Isl 4E 95
Culbo. High 3D 77
Culbokie. High 4D 77
Culburnie. High 1B 66
Culcabock. High 1D 67
Culcharry. High 4F 77
Culduie. High 1A 64
Culeave. High 4A 84
Culgaith. Cumb 4F 9
Culkein. High 4B 86
Culkein Drumbeg. High 4C 86
Cullen. Mor 3A 80
Cullicudden. High 3D 77
Cullipool. Arg 2E 37
Cullivoe. Shet 1H 101
Culloch. Per 2C 40
Culloden. High 1E 67
Cul na Caepaich. High 3F 53
Culnacnoc. High 3E 73
Culnacraig. High 3B 82
Culrain. High 4A 84
Culross. Fife 1B 32
Culroy. S Ayr 4E 19
Culswick. Shet 2A 100
Cults. Aber 1D 61
Cults. Abers 2A 70
Cults. Fife 3C 42
Cultybraggan Camp. Per 1C 40
Culzie Lodge. High 2C 76
**Cumbernauld**. N Lan 2F 31
Cumbernauld Village. N Lan 2F 31
Cumdivock. Cumb 3C 8
Cuminestown. Abers 4D 81
Cumledge Mill. Bord 4D 35
Cumlewick. Shet 4C 100
Cummersdale. Cumb 2C 8
Cummertrees. Dum 1A 8
Cummingstown. Mor 3C 78
Cumnock. E Ayr 3A 20
Cumrew. Cumb 2E 9
Cumwhinton. Cumb 2D 9
Cumwhitton. Cumb 2E 9
Cunninghamhead. N Ayr 1E 19
Cunning Park. S Ayr 4E 19
Cunningsburgh. Shet 4C 100
Cunnister. Shet 2H 101
Cupar. Fife 2C 42
Cupar Muir. Fife 2C 42
Currie. Edin 3D 33
Cuthill. E Lot 2F 33
Cutts. Shet 3B 100
Cuttyhill. Abers 4F 81


## D


Dacre. Cumb 4D 9
Dail. Arg 4B 46
Dail Beag. W Isl 2D 96
Dail bho Dheas. W Isl 1F 97
Dailly. S Ayr 1D 11
Dail Mor. W Isl 2D 96
Dairsie. Fife 2D 43
Dalabrog. W Isl 5G 93
Dalavich. Arg 2A 38
Dalbeattie. Dum 1D 7
Dalblair. E Ayr 4B 20
Dalchalm. High 3E 85
Dalcharn. High 2B 88
Dalchork. High 2A 84
Dalchreichart. High 4F 65
Dalchruin. Per 2C 40
Dalcross. High 1E 67
Dale. Cumb 3E 9
Dalelia. High 1E 45
Dale of Walls. Shet 1A 100
Dalgarven. N Ayr 1D 19
**Dalgety Bay**. Fife 1D 33
Dalginross. Per 1C 40
Dalguise. Per 3E 49
Dalhalvaig. High 2D 89
Dalintart. Arg 1F 37
**Dalkeith**. Midl 3F 33
Dallas. Mor 4C 78
Dalleagles. E Ayr 4A 20
Dall House. Per 2A 48
Dalmally. Arg 1C 38
Dalmarnock. Glas 3E 31
Dalmellington. E Ayr 1F 11
Dalmeny. Edin 2D 33
Dalmigavie. High 4E 67
Dalmilling. S Ayr 3E 19
Dalmore. High 3D 77
(nr. Alness)
Dalmore. High 3C 84
(nr. Rogart)
Dalmuir. W Dun 2C 30
Dalmunach. Mor 1D 69
Dalnabreck. High 1E 45
Dalnacardoch Lodge. Per 4E 57
Dalnamein Lodge. Per 1C 48
Dalnaspidal Lodge. Per 4D 57
Dalnatrat. High 2A 46
Dalnavie. High 2D 77
Dalnawillan Lodge. High 3F 89
Dalness. High 2C 46
Dalnessie. High 2B 84
Dalqueich. Per 3F 41
Dalquhairn. S Ayr 2E 11
Dalreavoch. High 3C 84
Dalreoch. Per 2F 41
Dalry. Edin 2E 33
Dalry. N Ayr 1D 19
Dalrymple. E Ayr 4E 19
Dalserf. S Lan 4A 32
Dalsmirren. Arg 4D 17

Dalston—Fitch


Dalston. *Cumb* 2C 8
Dalswinton. *Dum* 3E 13
Dalton. *Dum* 4A 14
Dalton. *S Lan* 4E 31
Daltot. *Arg* 1B 28
Dalvey. *High* 2C 68
Dalwhinnie. *High* 3D 57
Damhead. *Mor* 4B 78
Danderhall. *Midl* 3F 33
Danestone. *Aber* 4E 71
Dargill. *Per* 2D 41
Darnford. *Abers* 2C 60
Darnick. *Bord* 2E 23
Darra. *Abers* 1C 70
Dartfield. *Abers* 4F 81
Darvel. *E Ayr* 2A 20
Dava. *Mor* 2B 68
Davidson's Mains. *Edin* 2E 33
Davidston. *High* 3E 77
Davington. *Dum* 1B 14
Daviot. *Abers* 3C 70
Daviot. *High* 2E 67
Deadwater. *Nmbd* 2F 15
Dean. *Cumb* 4F 7
Deanburnhaugh. *Bord* 4C 22
Deanich Lodge. *High* 1A 76
Deans. *W Lot* 3C 32
Deanscales. *Cumb* 4F 7
Deanston. *Stir* 3C 40
Dearham. *Cumb* 4F 7
Dechmont. *W Lot* 2C 32
Deebank. *Abers* 2B 60
Deerhill. *Mor* 4F 79
Deerness. *Orkn* 2D 98
Delfour. *High* 1F 57
Delliefure. *High* 2B 68
Delny. *High* 2E 77
Den, The. *N Ayr* 4B 30
Denbeath. *Fife* 4C 42
Denhead. *Abers* 2E 71
(nr. Ellon)
Denhead. *Abers* 4E 81
(nr. Strichen)
Denhead. *Fife* 2D 43
Denholm. *Bord* 4E 23
**Denny**. *Falk* 1A 32
Dennyloanhead. *Falk* 1A 32
Den of Lindores. *Fife* 2B 42
Denside. *Abers* 2D 61
Denwick. *Nmbd* 4F 25
Derculich. *Per* 2D 49
Derryguaig. *Arg* 4B 44
Dervaig. *Arg* 2B 44
Detchant. *Nmbd* 2D 25
Deuchar. *Ang* 1D 51
Devonside. *Clac* 4E 41
Dewartown. *Midl* 3F 33
Digg. *High* 3D 73
Dillarburn. *S Lan* 1D 21
Dingleton. *Bord* 2E 23
Dingwall. *High* 4C 76
Dinnet. *Abers* 2F 59
Dippen. *Arg* 2E 17
Dippin. *N Ayr* 3B 18
Dipple. *S Ayr* 1D 11
Dirleton. *E Lot* 1B 34
Dishes. *Orkn* 5H 99
Distington. *Cumb* 4F 7
Divach. *High* 3B 66
Dixonfield. *High* 1A 90
Dochgarroch. *High* 1D 67
Doddington. *Nmbd* 2C 24
Doll. *High* 3D 85
Dollar. *Clac* 4E 41
Dolphinton. *S Lan* 1A 22
Doonfoot. *S Ayr* 4E 19
Doonholm. *S Ayr* 4E 19
Dorback Lodge. *High* 4B 68
Dores. *High* 2C 66
Dornie. *High* 3B 64
Dornoch. *High* 1E 77
Dornock. *Dum* 1B 8
Dorrery. *High* 2F 89
Dougarie. *N Ayr* 2F 17
Douglas. *S Lan* 2D 21
Douglastown. *Ang* 3D 51
Douglas Water. *S Lan* 2D 21
Dounby. *Orkn* 1A 98
Doune. *High* 4F 67
(nr. Kingussie)
Doune. *High* 3F 83
(nr. Lairg)
Doune. *Stir* 3C 40
Dounie. *High* 4A 84
(nr. Bonar Bridge)
Dounie. *High* 1D 77
(nr. Tain)
Dounreay. *High* 1E 89
Doura. *N Ayr* 1E 19
Dovenby. *Cumb* 4F 7
Dowally. *Per* 3F 49
Downfield. *D'dee* 4C 50
Downham. *Nmbd* 2B 24
Downies. *Abers* 2E 61
Doxford. *Nmbd* 3E 25
Draffan. *S Lan* 1C 20
Drakemyre. *N Ayr* 4A 30
Dreghorn. *N Ayr* 2E 19
Drem. *E Lot* 2B 34
Dreumasdal. *W Isl* 4G 93
Drimnin. *High* 2C 44
Drinisiadar. *W Isl* 3F 95
Droman. *High* 2C 86
Dron. *Per* 2A 42
Drongan. *E Ayr* 4F 19
Dronley. *Ang* 4C 50
Druim. *High* 4A 78
Druimarbin. *High* 4D 55
Druim Fhearna. *High* 4F 63
Druimindarroch. *High* 3F 53
Druim Saighdinis. *W Isl* 1H 93
Drum. *Per* 3F 41
Drumbeg. *High* 4C 86
Drumblade. *Abers* 1A 70
Drumbuie. *Dum* 3A 12
Drumbuie. *High* 2A 64
Drumburgh. *Cumb* 2B 8
Drumburn. *Dum* 1E 7
Drumchapel. *Glas* 2D 31
Drumchardine. *High* 1C 66
Drumchork. *High* 1B 74
Drumclog. *S Lan* 2B 20
Drumeldrie. *Fife* 3D 43
Drumelzier. *Bord* 2A 22
Drumfearn. *High* 4F 63
Drumgask. *High* 2D 57
Drumgelloch. *N Lan* 3F 31
Drumgley. *Ang* 2D 51
Drumguish. *High* 2E 57
Drumin. *Mor* 2C 68
Drumindorsair. *High* 1B 66
Drumlamford House. *S Ayr* 2B 4
Drumlasie. *Abers* 1B 60
Drumlemble. *Arg* 4D 17
Drumlithie. *Abers* 3C 60
Drummoddie. *Dum* 3E 5
Drummond. *High* 3D 77
Drummore. *Dum* 4C 4
Drummuir. *Mor* 1E 69
Drumnadrochit. *High* 2C 66
Drumnagorrach. *Mor* 4A 80
Drumoak. *Abers* 2C 60
Drumrunie. *High* 3C 82
Drumry. *W Dun* 2D 31
Drums. *Abers* 3E 71
Drumsleet. *Dum* 4E 13
Drumsmittal. *High* 1D 67
Drums of Park. *Abers* 4A 80
Drumsturdy. *Ang* 4D 51
Drumtochty Castle. *Abers* 3B 60
Drumuie. *High* 1D 63
Drumuillie. *High* 3A 68
Drumvaich. *Stir* 3B 40
Drumwhindle. *Abers* 2E 71
Drunkendub. *Ang* 3F 51
Drybridge. *Mor* 3F 79
Drybridge. *N Ayr* 2E 19
Dryburgh. *Bord* 2E 23
Drymen. *Stir* 1C 30
Drymuir. *Abers* 1E 71
Drynachan Lodge. *High* 2F 67
Drynie Park. *High* 4C 76
Drynoch. *High* 2D 63
Dubford. *Abers* 3C 80
Dubiton. *Abers* 4B 80
Dubton. *Ang* 2E 51
Duchally. *High* 2E 83
Duddingston. *Edin* 2E 33
Duddo. *Nmbd* 1C 24
Dufftown. *Mor* 1E 69
Duffus. *Mor* 3C 78
Dufton. *Cumb* 4F 9
Duirinish. *High* 2A 64
Duisdalemore. *High* 4F 63
Duisdeil Mòr. *High* 4F 63
Duisky. *High* 4D 55
Dull. *Per* 3D 49
Dullatur. *N Lan* 2F 31
Dulnain Bridge. *High* 3A 68
**Dumbarton**. *W Dun* 2C 30
Dumfin. *Arg* 1B 30
**Dumfries**. *Dum* 103 (4E 13)
Dumgoyne. *Stir* 1D 31
Dun. *Ang* 1F 51
Dunagoil. *Arg* 4E 29
Dunalastair. *Per* 2C 48
Dunan. *High* 3E 63
Dunbar. *E Lot* 2C 34
Dunbeath. *High* 4A 90
Dunbeg. *Arg* 4F 45
Dunblane. *Stir* 3C 40
Dunbog. *Fife* 2B 42
Duncanston. *Abers* 3A 70
Duncanston. *High* 4C 76
Dun Charlabhaigh. *W Isl* 2C 96
Duncow. *Dum* 3E 13
Duncrievie. *Per* 3A 42
**Dundee**. *D'dee* 103 (4D 51)
Dundee Airport. *D'dee* 1C 42
Dundonald. *S Ayr* 2E 19
Dundonnell. *High* 1D 75
Dundraw. *Cumb* 3B 8
Dundreggan. *High* 4A 66
Dundrennan. *Dum* 3C 6
Dunecht. *Abers* 1C 60
**Dunfermline**. *Fife* 103 (1C 32)
Dunino. *Fife* 2E 43
Dunipace. *Falk* 1A 32
Dunira. *Per* 1C 40
Dunkeld. *Per* 3F 49
Dunlappie. *Ang* 1E 51
Dunlichity Lodge. *High* 2D 67
Dunlop. *E Ayr* 1F 19
Dunmaglass Lodge. *High* 3C 66
Dunmore. *Arg* 3B 28
Dunmore. *Falk* 1A 32
Dunmore. *High* 1C 66
Dunnet. *High* 5A 98
Dunnichen. *Ang* 3E 51
Dunning. *Per* 2F 41
**Dunoon**. *Arg* 2F 29
Dunphail. *Mor* 1B 68
Dunragit. *Dum* 2C 4
Dunrostan. *Arg* 1B 28
Duns. *Bord* 4D 35
Dunscore. *Dum* 3D 13
Dunshalt. *Fife* 2B 42
Dunshillock. *Abers* 1E 71
Dunstan. *Nmbd* 4F 25
Dunsyre. *S Lan* 1F 21
Duntocher. *W Dun* 2C 30
Duntulm. *High* 2D 73
Dunure. *S Ayr* 4D 19
Dunvegan. *High* 1B 62
Durdar. *Cumb* 2D 9
Durisdeer. *Dum* 1D 13
Durisdeermill. *Dum* 1D 13
Durnamuck. *High* 4B 82
Durness. *High* 1F 87
Durno. *Abers* 3C 70
Duror. *High* 2A 46
Durran. *Arg* 3A 38
Durran. *High* 1A 90
Dury. *Shet* 1C 100
Duthil. *High* 3A 68
Dyce. *Aber* 4D 71
Dyke. *Mor* 4A 78
Dykehead. *Ang* 1C 50
Dykehead. *N Lan* 3A 32
Dykehead. *Stir* 4A 40
Dykend. *Ang* 2B 50
Dykesfield. *Cumb* 2C 8
Dysart. *Fife* 4C 42


## E


Eadar Dha Fhadhail. *W Isl* 3B 96
Eaglesfield. *Cumb* 4F 7
Eaglesfield. *Dum* 4B 14
Eaglesham. *E Ren* 4D 31
Eallabus. *Arg* 3D 27
Eals. *Nmbd* 2F 9
Eamont Bridge. *Cumb* 4E 9
Earlais. *High* 3C 72
Earle. *Nmbd* 3C 24
Earlish. *High* 3C 72
Earlsferry. *Fife* 3D 43
Earlsford. *Abers* 2D 71
Earlston. *E Ayr* 2F 19
Earlston. *Bord* 2E 23
Earlstoun. *Dum* 3B 12
Earlyvale. *Bord* 4E 33
Earsairidh. *W Isl* 3C 92
Easdale. *Arg* 2E 37
Easington. *Nmbd* 2E 25
Eassie. *Ang* 3C 50
Eassie and Nevay. *Ang* 3C 50
East Barns. *E Lot* 2D 35
East Bennan. *N Ayr* 3A 18
East Bolton. *Nmbd* 4E 25
East Burrafirth. *Shet* 1B 100
East Calder. *W Lot* 3C 32
East Clyne. *High* 3D 85
East Clyth. *High* 4B 90
East Croachy. *High* 3D 67
Easter Ardross. *High* 2D 77
Easter Balgedie. *Per* 3A 42
Easter Balmoral. *Abers* 2D 59
Easter Brae. *High* 3D 77
Easter Buckieburn. *Stir* 1F 31
Easter Fearn. *High* 1D 77
Easter Galcantray. *High* 1F 67
Easterhouse. *Glas* 3E 31
Easter Howgate. *Midl* 3E 33
Easter Kinkell. *High* 4C 76
Easter Lednathie. *Ang* 1C 50
Easter Ogil. *Ang* 1D 51
Easter Ord. *Abers* 1D 61
Easter Quarff. *Shet* 3C 100
Easter Rhynd. *Per* 2A 42
Easter Skeld. *Shet* 2B 100
Easter Suddie. *High* 4D 77
Easter Tulloch. *Abers* 4C 60
Eastfield. *N Lan* 3A 32
(nr. Caldercruix)
Eastfield. *N Lan* 3A 32
(nr. Harthill)
Eastfield. *S Lan* 3E 31
Eastfield Hall. *Nmbd* 4F 25
East Fortune. *E Lot* 2B 34
East Haven. *Ang* 4E 51
East Helmsdale. *High* 2F 85
East Horton. *Nmbd* 2D 25
Easthouses. *Midl* 3F 33
**East Kilbride**. *S Lan* 4E 31
East Kyloe. *Nmbd* 2D 25
East Langwell. *High* 3C 84
East Learmouth. *Nmbd* 2B 24
East Lilburn. *Nmbd* 3D 25
East Linton. *E Lot* 2B 34
East Mains. *Abers* 2B 60
East Mey. *High* 5B 98
Easton. *Cumb* 2B 8
(nr. Burgh by Sands)
Easton. *Cumb* 4D 15
(nr. Longtown)
East Ord. *Nmbd* 4F 35
East Pitcorthie. *Fife* 3E 43
East Rhidorroch Lodge. *High* 4D 83
Eastriggs. *Dum* 1B 8
East Saltoun. *E Lot* 3A 34
Eastshore. *Shet* 5B 100
East Wemyss. *Fife* 4C 42
East Whitburn. *W Lot* 3B 32
Eastwick. *Shet* 4F 101
Ecclefechan. *Dum* 4A 14
Eccles. *Bord* 1A 24
Ecclesmachan. *W Lot* 2C 32
Echt. *Abers* 1C 60
Eckford. *Bord* 3A 24
Eday Airport. *Orkn* 4G 99
Edderside. *Cumb* 3A 8
Edderton. *High* 1E 77
Eddleston. *Bord* 1B 22
Eddlewood. *S Lan* 4F 31
Edendonich. *Arg* 1C 38
Edenhall. *Cumb* 4E 9
Edentaggart. *Arg* 4E 39
Edgehead. *Midl* 3F 33
Edinbane. *High* 4C 72
**Edinburgh**. *Edin* 104 (2E 33)
Edinburgh Airport. *Edin* 2D 33
Edlingham. *Nmbd* 4E 25
Edmonstone. *Orkn* 5G 99
Ednam. *Bord* 2A 24
Edrom. *Bord* 4E 35
Edzell. *Ang* 1F 51
Effirth. *Shet* 1B 100
Efstigarth. *Shet* 2G 101
Eglingham. *Nmbd* 4E 25
Eight Mile Burn. *Midl* 4D 33
Eignaig. *High* 3E 45
Eilanreach. *High* 4B 64
Eildon. *Bord* 2E 23
Eileanach Lodge. *High* 3C 76
Eilean Fhlodaigh. *W Isl* 2H 93
Eilean Iarmain. *High* 4A 64
Einacleit. *W Isl* 4C 96
Eisgein. *W Isl* 1H 95
Elcho. *Per* 1A 42
Elderslie. *Ren* 3C 30
Elford. *Nmbd* 2E 25
**Elgin**. *Mor* 3D 79
Elgol. *High* 4E 63
Elie. *Fife* 3D 43
Elizafield. *Dum* 4F 13
Ellan. *High* 3F 67
Ellary. *Arg* 2B 28
Ellemford. *Bord* 3D 35
Ellenabeich. *Arg* 2E 37
Ellenborough. *Cumb* 4F 7
Elleric. *Arg* 3B 46
Ellingham. *Nmbd* 3E 25
Elliot. *Ang* 4F 51
Ellishadder. *High* 3E 73
Ellon. *Abers* 2E 71
Ellonby. *Cumb* 4D 9
Elphin. *High* 2D 83
Elphinstone. *E Lot* 2F 33
Elrick. *Abers* 1D 61
Elrick. *Mor* 3F 69
Elrig. *Dum* 3E 5
Elsrickle. *S Lan* 1F 21
Elvanfoot. *S Lan* 4E 21
Elvingston. *E Lot* 2A 34
Elwick. *Nmbd* 2E 25
Embleton. *Cumb* 4A 8
Embleton. *Nmbd* 3F 25
Embo. *High* 4D 85
Embo Street. *High* 4D 85
Enoch. *Dum* 1D 13
Enochdhu. *Per* 1F 49
Ensay. *Arg* 3A 44
Enterkinfoot. *Dum* 1D 13
Eolaigearraidh. *W Isl* 2C 92
Eorabus. *Arg* 1A 36
Eoropaidh. *W Isl* 1G 97
Erbusaig. *High* 3A 64
Erchless Castle. *High* 1B 66
Eredine. *Arg* 3A 38
Eriboll. *High* 2F 87
Ericstane. *Dum* 4F 21
Erines. *Arg* 2C 28
Errogie. *High* 3C 66
Errol. *Per* 1B 42
Errol Station. *Per* 1B 42
**Erskine**. *Ren* 2C 30
**Erskine Bridge**. *Ren* 2C 30
Ervie. *Dum* 1B 4
Eskadale. *High* 2B 66
Eskbank. *Midl* 3F 33
Eskdalemuir. *Dum* 2B 14
Esknish. *Arg* 3D 27
Eslington Hall. *Nmbd* 4D 25
Essich. *High* 2D 67
Eswick. *Shet* 1C 100
Etal. *Nmbd* 2C 24
Ethie Haven. *Ang* 3F 51
Etteridge. *High* 2D 57
Ettrick. *Bord* 4B 22
Ettrickbridge. *Bord* 3C 22
Evanton. *High* 3D 77
Evelix. *High* 4C 84
Everbay. *Orkn* 5H 99
Evertown. *Dum* 4C 14
Ewes. *Dum* 2C 14
Exnaboe. *Shet* 5B 100
Eyemouth. *Bord* 3F 35
Eynort. *High* 3C 62
Eyre. *High* 4D 73
(on Isle of Skye)
Eyre. *High* 2E 63
(on Raasay)


## F


Faichem. *High* 1F 55
Faifley. *W Dun* 2D 31
Fail. *S Ayr* 3F 19
Failford. *S Ayr* 3F 19
Fair Hill. *Cumb* 4E 9
Fairhill. *S Lan* 4F 31
Fair Isle Airport. *Shet* 1H 99
Fairlie. *N Ayr* 4A 30
Fairmilehead. *Edin* 3E 33
Fala. *Midl* 3A 34
Fala Dam. *Midl* 3A 34
**Falkirk**. *Falk* 105 (1A 32)
Falkland. *Fife* 3B 42
Fallin. *Stir* 4D 41
Falstone. *Nmbd* 3F 15
Fanagmore. *High* 3C 86
Fanellan. *High* 1B 66
Fankerton. *Falk* 1F 31
Fanmore. *Arg* 3B 44
Fannich Lodge. *High* 3F 75
Fans. *Bord* 1F 23
Farlam. *Cumb* 2E 9
Farley. *High* 1B 66
Farmtown. *Mor* 4A 80
Farnell. *Ang* 2F 51
Farr. *High* 1C 88
(nr. Bettyhill)
Farr. *High* 2D 67
(nr. Inverness)
Farr. *High* 1F 57
(nr. Kingussie)
Farraline. *High* 3C 66
Fasag. *High* 4B 74
Fascadale. *High* 4E 53
Fasnacloich. *Arg* 3B 46
Fassfern. *High* 4D 55
Faugh. *Cumb* 2E 9
Fauldhouse. *W Lot* 3B 32
Feagour. *High* 2C 56
Fearann Dhomhnaill. *High* 1F 53
Fearn. *High* 2F 77
Fearnan. *Per* 3C 48
Fearnbeg. *High* 4A 74
Fearnmore. *High* 3A 74
Featherstone Castle. *Nmbd* 1F 9
Felkington. *Nmbd* 1C 24
Fell Side. *Cumb* 4C 8
Fenham. *Nmbd* 1D 25
Fenton. *Cumb* 2E 9
Fenton. *Nmbd* 2C 24
Fenton Barns. *E Lot* 1B 34
Fenwick. *E Ayr* 1F 19
Fenwick. *Nmbd* 1D 25
Feochaig. *Arg* 4E 17
Feolin Ferry. *Arg* 3E 27
Feorlan. *Arg* 4D 17
Ferindonald. *High* 1F 53
Feriniquarrie. *High* 4A 72
Fern. *Ang* 1D 51
Ferness. *High* 1A 68
Fernieflatt. *Abers* 4D 61
Ferniegair. *S Lan* 4F 31
Fernilea. *High* 2C 62
Ferryden. *Ang* 2F 51
Ferryhill. *Aber* 1E 61
Ferryton. *High* 3D 77
Fersit. *High* 4A 56
Feshiebridge. *High* 1F 57
Fetterangus. *Abers* 4E 81
Fettercairn. *Abers* 4B 60
Fiag Lodge. *High* 1F 83
Fidden. *Arg* 1A 36
Fieldhead. *Cumb* 4D 9
Fife Keith. *Mor* 4F 79
Finavon. *Ang* 2D 51
Fincharn. *Arg* 3A 38
Findhorn. *Mor* 3B 78
Findhorn Bridge. *High* 3F 67
Findochty. *Mor* 3F 79
Findo Gask. *Per* 1F 41
Findon. *Abers* 2E 61
Findon Mains. *High* 3D 77
Fingland. *Cumb* 2B 8
Fingland. *Dum* 4C 20
Finiskaig. *High* 2B 54
Finnart. *Per* 2A 48
Finnygaud. *Abers* 4B 80
Finstown. *Orkn* 1B 98
Fintry. *Abers* 4C 80
Fintry. *D'dee* 4D 51
Fintry. *Stir* 1E 31
Finzean. *Abers* 2B 60
Fionnphort. *Arg* 1A 36
Fionnsabhagh. *W Isl* 4E 95
First Coast. *High* 4A 82
Firth. *Shet* 4G 101
Fishcross. *Clac* 4D 41
Fisherford. *Abers* 2B 70
Fisherrow. *E Lot* 2F 33
Fisherton. *High* 4E 77
Fisherton. *S Ayr* 4D 19
Fishnish. *Arg* 3D 45
Fishwick. *Bord* 4F 35
Fiskavaig. *High* 2C 62
Fitch. *Shet* 2B 100

Fiunary—Haugh of Urr


Fiunary. *High* 3D **45**
Fladda. *Shet* 3F **101**
Fladdabister. *Shet* 3C **100**
Flashader. *High* 4C **72**
Flatt, The. *Cumb* 4E **15**
Fleck. *Shet* 5B **100**
Fleisirin. *W Isl* 3G **97**
Flemington. *S Lan* 3E **31**
(nr. Glasgow)
Flemington. *S Lan* 1C **20**
(nr. Strathaven)
Fleoideabhagh. *W Isl* 4E **95**
Fletchertown. *Cumb* 3B **8**
Fleuchary. *High* 4C **84**
Flimby. *Cumb* 4F **7**
Flodden. *Nmbd* 2C **24**
Flodigarry. *High* 2D **73**
Flushing. *Abers* 1F **71**
Fochabers. *Mor* 4E **79**
Fodderty. *High* 4C **76**
Foffarty. *Ang* 3D **51**
Fogo. *Bord* 1A **24**
Fogorig. *Bord* 1A **24**
Foindle. *High* 3C **86**
Folda. *Ang* 1A **50**
Folla Rule. *Abers* 2C **70**
Foodieash. *Fife* 2C **42**
Footdee. *Aber* 1E **61**
Forbestown. *Abers* 4E **69**
Ford. *Arg* 3F **37**
Ford. *Nmbd* 2C **24**
Fordell. *Fife* 1D **33**
Fordie. *Per* 1C **40**
Fordoun. *Abers* 4C **60**
Fordyce. *Abers* 3A **80**
Foresterseat. *Mor* 4C **78**
Forest Head. *Cumb* 2E **9**
Forest Lodge. *Per* 4A **58**
Forest Mill. *Clac* 4E **41**
**Forfar**. *Ang* 2D **51**
Forgandenny. *Per* 2F **41**
Forgewood. *N Lan* 4F **31**
Forgie. *Mor* 4E **79**
Forgue. *Abers* 1B **70**
Forneth. *Per* 3F **49**
Forres. *Mor* 4B **78**
Forrestfield. *N Lan* 3A **32**
Forrest Lodge. *Dum* 3A **12**
Forse. *High* 4B **90**
Forsinard. *High* 3D **89**
Forss. *High* 1F **89**
Fort Augustus. *High* 1A **56**
Forteviot. *Per* 2F **41**
Fort George. *High* 4E **77**
Forth. *S Lan* 4B **32**
Forth Road Bridge.
*Edin* 2D **33**
Fortingall. *Per* 3C **48**
Fort Matilda. *Inv* 2A **30**
Fortrie. *Abers* 1B **70**
Fortrose. *High* 4E **77**
**Fort William**. *High* **105** (4E **55**)
Foss. *Per* 2C **48**
Fothergill. *Cumb* 4F **7**
Foubister. *Orkn* 2D **98**
Foula Airport. *Shet* 4A **100**
Foulbridge. *Cumb* 3D **9**
Foulden. *Bord* 4F **35**
Fountainhall. *Bord* 1D **23**
Foveran. *Abers* 3E **71**
Fowlershill. *Aber* 4E **71**
Fowlis. *Ang* 4C **50**
Fowlis Wester. *Per* 1E **41**
Foyers. *High* 3B **66**
Foynesfield. *High* 4F **77**
**Fraserburgh**. *Abers* 3E **81**
Freester. *Shet* 1C **100**
Frenich. *Stir* 3F **39**
Fresgoe. *High* 1E **89**
Freswick. *High* 1C **90**
Freuchie. *Fife* 3B **42**
Friockheim. *Ang* 3E **51**
Frobost. *W Isl* 5G **93**
Frotoft. *Orkn* 5F **99**
Fullwood. *E Ayr* 4C **30**
Funzie. *Shet* 2H **101**
Furnace. *Arg* 3B **38**
Fyvie. *Abers* 2C **70**


## G


Gabhsann bho Dheas. *W Isl* 1F **97**
Gabhsann bho Thuath.
*W Isl* 1F **97**
Gabroc Hill. *E Ayr* 4C **30**
Gadgirth. *S Ayr* 3F **19**
Gaick Lodge. *High* 3E **57**
Gairletter. *Arg* 1F **29**
Gairloch. *Abers* 1C **60**
Gairloch. *High* 2B **74**
Gairlochy. *High* 3E **55**
Gairney Bank. *Per* 4A **42**
Gairnshiel Lodge. *Abers* 1D **59**
Gaitsgill. *Cumb* 3C **8**
**Galashiels**. *Bord* 2D **23**
Gallatown. *Fife* 4B **42**
Gallin. *Per* 3A **48**
Gallowfauld. *Ang* 3D **51**
Gallowhill. *Per* 4A **50**
Gallowhill. *Ren* 3C **30**
Gallowhills. *Abers* 4F **81**
Galltair. *High* 3B **64**
Galmisdale. *High* 3D **53**
Galston. *E Ayr* 2F **19**
Galtrigill. *High* 4A **72**
Gamblesby. *Cumb* 4F **9**
Gamelsby. *Cumb* 2B **8**
Ganavan. *Arg* 4F **45**
Gannochy. *Ang* 4A **60**
Gannochy. *Per* 1A **42**
Gansclet. *High* 3C **90**
Garafad. *High* 3D **73**
Gardenstown. *Abers* 3D **81**
Garderhouse. *Shet* 2B **100**
Gardie Ho. *Shet* 2C **100**
Garelochhead. *Arg* 4D **39**
Gargunnock. *Stir* 4C **40**
Garleffin. *S Ayr* 3B **10**
Garlieston. *Dum* 3F **5**
Garlogie. *Abers* 1C **60**
Garmond. *Abers* 4D **81**
Garmony. *Arg* 3D **45**
Garmouth. *Mor* 3E **79**
Garnkirk. *N Lan* 3E **31**
Garrabost. *W Isl* 3G **97**
Garrallan. *E Ayr* 4A **20**
Garrigill. *Cumb* 3F **9**
Garrogie Lodge. *High* 4C **66**
Garros. *High* 3D **73**
Garrow. *Per* 3D **49**
Gartcosh. *N Lan* 3E **31**
Garth. *Shet* 1A **100**
(nr. Sandness)
Garth. *Shet* 1C **100**
(nr. Skellister)
Garthamlock. *Glas* 3E **31**
Gartly. *Abers* 2A **70**
Gartmore. *Stir* 4A **40**
Gartness. *N Lan* 3F **31**
Gartness. *Stir* 1D **31**
Gartocharn. *W Dun* 1C **30**
Gartsherrie. *N Lan* 3F **31**
Gartymore. *High* 2F **85**
Garvald. *E Lot* 2B **34**
Garvamore. *High* 2C **56**
Garvard. *Arg* 4A **36**
Garvault. *High* 4C **88**
Garve. *High* 3A **76**
Garvie. *Arg* 4B **38**
Garvock. *Abers* 4C **60**
Garvock. *Inv* 2A **30**
Gaskan. *High* 4B **54**
Gatehead. *E Ayr* 2E **19**
Gatehouse of Fleet. *Dum* 2B **6**
Gatelawbridge. *Dum* 2E **13**
Gateside. *Ang* 3D **51**
(nr. Forfar)
Gateside. *Ang* 3C **50**
(nr. Kirriemuir)
Gateside. *Fife* 3A **42**
Gateside. *N Ayr* 4B **30**
Gattonside. *Bord* 2E **23**
Gauldry. *Fife* 1C **42**
Gavinton. *Bord* 4D **35**
Gayfield. *Orkn* 2F **99**
Geanies. *High* 2F **77**
Gearraidh Bhailteas. *W Isl* 5G **93**
Gearraidh Bhaird. *W Isl* 1H **95**
Gearraidh ma Monadh.
*W Isl* 1C **92**
Gearraidh na h-Aibhne.
*W Isl* 3D **96**
Geary. *High* 3B **72**
Geddes. *High* 4F **77**
Gedintailor. *High* 2E **63**
Geilston. *Arg* 2B **30**
Geirinis. *W Isl* 3G **93**
Geise. *High* 1A **90**
Geisiadar. *W Isl* 3C **96**
Gelder Shiel. *Abers* 3D **59**
Gellyburn. *Per* 4F **49**
Gelston. *Dum* 2C **6**
Geocrab. *W Isl* 3F **95**
Georgetown. *Ren* 3C **30**
Georth. *Orkn* 5E **99**
Gerston. *High* 2A **90**
**Giffnock**. *E Ren* 4D **31**
Gifford. *E Lot* 3B **34**
Giffordtown. *Fife* 2B **42**
Gilchriston. *E Lot* 3A **34**
Gilcrux. *Cumb* 4A **8**
Gillen. *High* 4B **72**
Gillock. *High* 2B **90**
Gills. *High* 5B **98**
Gilmanscleuch. *Bord* 3C **22**
Gilmerton. *Edin* 3E **33**
Gilmerton. *Per* 1D **41**
Gilsland. *Nmbd* 1F **9**
Gilsland Spa. *Cumb* 1F **9**
Gilston. *Bord* 4A **34**
Giosla. *W Isl* 4C **96**
Girdle Toll. *N Ayr* 1E **19**
Girlsta. *Shet* 1C **100**
Girthon. *Dum* 2B **6**
Girvan. *S Ayr* 2C **10**
Gladsmuir. *E Lot* 2A **34**
Glaichbea. *High* 2C **66**
Glame. *High* 1E **63**
Glamis. *Ang* 3C **50**
Glanton. *Nmbd* 4D **25**
Glanton Pyke. *Nmbd* 4D **25**
Glas Aird. *Arg* 4A **36**
Glas-allt Shiel. *Abers* 3D **59**
Glaschoil. *High* 2B **68**
**Glasgow**. *Glas* **104** (3D **31**)
Glasgow Airport. *Ren* 3C **30**
Glasgow Prestwick Airport.
*S Ayr* 3E **19**
Glashvin. *High* 3D **73**
Glas na Cardaich. *High* 2F **53**
Glasnacardoch. *High* 2F **53**
Glasnakille. *High* 4E **63**
Glassburn. *High* 2A **66**
Glasserton. *Dum* 4F **5**
Glassford. *S Lan* 1C **20**
Glassgreen. *Mor* 3D **79**
Glasson. *Cumb* 1B **8**
Glassonby. *Cumb* 4E **9**
Glasterlaw. *Ang* 2E **51**
Gleann Dail bho Dheas.
*W Isl* 1C **92**
Gleann Tholastaidh. *W Isl* 2G **97**
Gleann Uige. *High* 4F **53**
Glecknabae. *Arg* 3E **29**
Glen. *Dum* 2A **6**
Glenancross. *High* 2F **53**
Glenbarr. *Arg* 2D **17**
Glenbeg. *High* 1C **44**
Glen Bernisdale. *High* 1D **63**
Glenbervie. *Abers* 3C **60**
Glenboig. *N Lan* 3F **31**
Glenborrodale. *High* 1D **45**
Glenbranter. *Arg* 4C **38**
Glenbreck. *Bord* 3F **21**
Glenbrein Lodge. *High* 4B **66**
Glenbrittle. *High* 3D **63**
Glenbuchat Lodge. *Abers* 4E **69**
Glenbuck. *E Ayr* 3C **20**
Glenburn. *Ren* 3C **30**
Glencalvie Lodge. *High* 1B **76**
Glencaple. *Dum* 1E **7**
Glencarron Lodge. *High* 4D **75**
Glencarse. *Per* 1A **42**
Glencassley Castle. *High* 3F **83**
Glencat. *Abers* 2A **60**
Glencoe. *High* 2C **46**
Glen Cottage. *High* 3F **53**
Glencraig. *Fife* 4A **42**
Glendale. *High* 1A **62**
Glendevon. *Per* 3E **41**
Glendoebeg. *High* 1B **56**
Glendoick. *Per* 1B **42**
Glendoune. *S Ayr* 2C **10**
Glenduckie. *Fife* 2B **42**
Gleneagles. *Per* 3E **41**
Glenegedale. *Arg* 4D **27**
Glenegedale Lots. *Arg* 4D **27**
Glenelg. *High* 4B **64**
Glenernie. *Mor* 1B **68**
Glenesslin. *Dum* 3D **13**
Glenfarg. *Per* 2A **42**
Glenfarquhar Lodge. *Abers* 3C **60**
Glenferness Mains. *High* 1A **68**
Glenfeshie Lodge. *High* 2F **57**
Glenfiddich Lodge. *Mor* 2E **69**
Glenfinnan. *High* 3C **54**
Glenfintaig Lodge. *High* 3F **55**
Glenfoot. *Per* 2A **42**
Glenfyne Lodge. *Arg* 2D **39**
Glengap. *Dum* 2B **6**
Glengarnock. *N Ayr* 4B **30**
Glengolly. *High* 1A **90**
Glengorm Castle. *Arg* 2B **44**
Glengrasco. *High* 1D **63**
Glenhead Farm. *Ang* 1B **50**
Glenholm. *Bord* 2A **22**
Glen House. *Bord* 2B **22**
Glenhurich. *High* 1F **45**
Glenkerry. *Bord* 4B **22**
Glenkiln. *Dum* 4D **13**
Glenkindie. *Abers* 4F **69**
Glenkinglass Lodge. *Arg* 4C **46**
Glenkirk. *Bord* 3F **21**
Glenlean. *Arg* 1E **29**
Glenlee. *Dum* 3B **12**
Glenleraig. *High* 4C **86**
Glenlichorn. *Per* 2C **40**
Glenlivet. *Mor* 3C **68**
Glenlochar. *Dum* 1C **6**
Glenlochsie Lodge. *Per* 4B **58**
Glenluce. *Dum* 2C **4**
Glenmarksie. *High* 4A **76**
Glenmassan. *Arg* 1F **29**
Glenmavis. *N Lan* 3F **31**
Glenmazeran Lodge. *High* 3E **67**
Glenmidge. *Dum* 3D **13**
Glenmore. *High* 1C **44**
(nr. Glenborrodale)
Glenmore. *High* 1A **58**
(nr. Kingussie)
Glenmore. *High* 1D **63**
(on Isle of Skye)
Glenmoy. *Ang* 1D **51**
Glennoe. *Arg* 4B **46**
Glen of Coachford. *Abers* 1F **69**
Glenogil. *Ang* 1D **51**
Glenprosen Village. *Ang* 1C **50**
Glenree. *N Ayr* 3A **18**
Glenrosa. *N Ayr* 2B **18**
**Glenrothes**. *Fife* 3B **42**
Glensanda. *High* 3F **45**
Glensaugh. *Abers* 4B **60**
Glenshero Lodge. *High* 2C **56**
Glensluain. *Arg* 4B **38**
Glenstockadale. *Dum* 1B **4**
Glenstriven. *Arg* 2E **29**
Glen Tanar House. *Abers* 2F **59**
Glenton. *Abers* 3B **70**
Glentress. *Bord* 2B **22**
Glentromie Lodge. *High* 2E **57**
Glentrool Lodge. *Dum* 3F **11**
Glentrool Village. *Dum* 4E **11**
Glentruim House. *High* 2D **57**
Glenuig. *High* 4F **53**
Glen Village. *Falk* 2A **32**
Glenwhilly. *Dum* 4C **10**
Glenzierfoot. *Dum* 4C **14**
Glespin. *S Lan* 3D **21**
Gletness. *Shet* 1C **100**
Glib Cheois. *W Isl* 4E **97**
Gloster Hill. *Nmbd* 4F **25**
Gloup. *Shet* 1H **101**
Glutt Lodge. *High* 4E **89**
Gobernuisgach Lodge. *High* 3F **87**
Gobernuisgeach. *High* 4E **89**
Gobhaig. *W Isl* 2E **95**
Gogar. *Edin* 2D **33**
Gollanfield. *High* 4F **77**
Golspie. *High* 4D **85**
Gometra House. *Arg* 3A **44**
Gonfirth. *Shet* 5F **101**
Gord. *Shet* 4C **100**
Gordon. *Bord* 1F **23**
Gordonbush. *High* 3D **85**
Gordonstown. *Abers* 4A **80**
(nr. Cornhill)
Gordonstown. *Abers* 2C **70**
(nr. Fyvie)
Gorebridge. *Midl* 3F **33**
Gorgie. *Edin* 2E **33**
Gorseness. *Orkn* 1C **98**
Gorstan. *High* 3A **76**
Gortantaoid. *Arg* 2D **27**
Gorteneorn. *High* 1D **45**
Gortenfern. *High* 1D **45**
Gossabrough. *Shet* 3H **101**
Goswick. *Nmbd* 1D **25**
Gott. *Arg* 3F **91**
Gott. *Shet* 2C **100**
Gourdon. *Abers* 4D **61**
Gourock. *Inv* 2A **30**
Govan. *Glas* 3D **31**
Govanhill. *Glas* 3D **31**
Gowanhill. *Abers* 3F **81**
Gowkhall. *Fife* 1C **32**
Grabhair. *W Isl* 1H **95**
Gramasdail. *W Isl* 2H **93**
Grandtully. *Per* 2E **49**
Grange. *E Ayr* 2F **19**
Grange. *Per* 1B **42**
Grange Crossroads. *Mor* 4F **79**
**Grangemouth**. *Falk* 1B **32**
Grange of Lindores. *Fife* 2B **42**
Grangepans. *Falk* 1C **32**
Granish. *High* 4F **67**
Grantlodge. *Abers* 4C **70**
Granton. *Edin* 2E **33**
Grantown-on-Spey. *High* 3B **68**
Grantshouse. *Bord* 3E **35**
Grassgarth. *Cumb* 3C **8**
Graven. *Shet* 4G **101**
Grayson Green. *Cumb* 4E **7**
Grealin. *High* 3E **73**
Great Blencow. *Cumb* 4D **9**
Great Broughton. *Cumb* 4F **7**
Great Clifton. *Cumb* 4F **7**
Great Corby. *Cumb* 2D **9**
Great Orton. *Cumb* 2C **8**
Great Ryle. *Nmbd* 4D **25**
Great Salkeld. *Cumb* 4E **9**
Greenbank. *Shet* 1H **101**
Greenburn. *W Lot* 3B **32**
Greendykes. *Nmbd* 3D **25**
Greenfield. *Arg* 4D **39**
Greenfoot. *N Lan* 3F **31**
Greengairs. *N Lan* 2F **31**
Greengill. *Cumb* 4A **8**
Greenhead. *Nmbd* 1F **9**
Greenhill. *Dum* 4A **14**
Greenhill. *Falk* 2A **32**
Greenhills. *N Ayr* 4B **30**
Greenholm. *E Ayr* 2A **20**
Greenigoe. *Orkn* 2C **98**
Greenland. *High* 1B **90**
Greenland Mains. *High* 1B **90**
Greenlaw. *Bord* 1A **24**
Greenlea. *Dum* 4F **13**
Greenloaning. *Per* 3D **41**
Greenmow. *Shet* 4C **100**
**Greenock**. *Inv* 2A **30**
Greenock Mains. *E Ayr* 3B **20**
Greenrow. *Cumb* 2A **8**
Greens. *Abers* 1D **71**
Greensidehill. *Nmbd* 4C **24**
Greenwall. *Orkn* 2D **98**
Greenwell. *Cumb* 2E **9**
Grein. *W Isl* 2B **92**
Greinetobht. *W Isl* 5C **94**
Gremista. *Shet* 2C **100**
Greosabhagh. *W Isl* 3F **95**
Greshornish. *High* 4C **72**
Gretna. *Dum* 1C **8**
Gretna Green. *Dum* 1C **8**
Greysouthen. *Cumb* 4F **7**
Greystoke. *Cumb* 4D **9**
Greystoke Gill. *Cumb* 4D **9**
Greystone. *Ang* 3E **51**
Griais. *W Isl* 2F **97**
Grianan. *W Isl* 3F **97**
Gribun. *Arg* 4B **44**
Grimbister. *Orkn* 1B **98**
Grimeston. *Orkn* 1B **98**
Griminis. *W Isl* 2G **93**
(on Benbecula)
Griminis. *W Isl* 5B **94**
(on North Uist)
Grimister. *Shet* 2G **101**
Grimness. *Orkn* 3C **98**
Grindiscol. *Shet* 3C **100**
Grindon. *Nmbd* 1C **24**
Grinsdale. *Cumb* 2C **8**
Griomsidar. *W Isl* 4F **97**
Grishipoll. *Arg* 2G **91**
Gritley. *Orkn* 2D **98**
Grobister. *Orkn* 5H **99**
Grobsness. *Shet* 5F **101**
Grogport. *Arg* 1F **17**
Groigearraidh. *W Isl* 3G **93**
Grove, The. *Dum* 4E **13**
Grudie. *High* 3A **76**
Gruids. *High* 3A **84**
Gruinard House. *High* 4A **82**
Gruinart. *Arg* 3C **26**
Grulinbeg. *Arg* 3C **26**
Gruline. *Arg* 3C **44**
Grummore. *High* 4B **88**
Gruting. *Shet* 2A **100**
Grutness. *Shet* 5C **100**
Gualachulain. *High* 3C **46**
Gualin House. *High* 2E **87**
Guardbridge. *Fife* 2D **43**
Guay. *Per* 3F **49**
Guildtown. *Per* 4A **50**
Gulberwick. *Shet* 3C **100**
Gullane. *E Lot* 1A **34**
Gunnista. *Shet* 2C **100**
Gunsgreenhill. *Bord* 3F **35**
Gutcher. *Shet* 2H **101**
Guthrie. *Ang* 2E **51**
Guyzance. *Nmbd* 4F **25**


## H


Haa of Houlland. *Shet* 1H **101**
Hackland. *Orkn* 5E **99**
Hackness. *Orkn* 3B **98**
Haclait. *W Isl* 3H **93**
Hadden. *Bord* 2A **24**
Haddington. *E Lot* 2B **34**
Haddo. *Abers* 2D **71**
Haggbeck. *Cumb* 4D **15**
Haggersta. *Shet* 2B **100**
Haggerston. *Nmbd* 1D **25**
Haggrister. *Shet* 4F **101**
Halbeath. *Fife* 1D **33**
Halcro. *High* 1B **90**
Halistra. *High* 4B **72**
Halket. *E Ayr* 4C **30**
Halkirk. *High* 2A **90**
Hall. *E Ren* 4C **30**
Hallbankgate. *Cumb* 2E **9**
Halliburton. *Bord* 1F **23**
Hallin. *High* 4B **72**
Hallyne. *Bord* 1A **22**
Haltcliff Bridge. *Cumb* 4C **8**
Halton Lea Gate. *Nmbd* 2F **9**
Haltwhistle. *Nmbd* 1F **9**
Ham. *High* 5A **98**
Ham. *Shet* 4A **100**
**Hamilton**. *S Lan* **105** (4F **31**)
Hamister. *Shet* 5H **101**
Hamnavoe. *Shet* 3E **101**
(nr. Braehoulland)
Hamnavoe. *Shet* 3B **100**
(nr. Burland)
Hamnavoe. *Shet* 4G **101**
(nr. Lunna)
Hamnavoe. *Shet* 3G **101**
(on Yell)
Happas. *Ang* 3D **51**
Happendon. *S Lan* 2D **21**
Harbottle. *Nmbd* 4C **24**
Hardgate. *Abers* 1C **60**
Hardgate. *Dum* 1D **7**
Harehope. *Nmbd* 3D **25**
Harelaw. *Dum* 4D **15**
Haresceugh. *Cumb* 3F **9**
Hareshaw. *N Lan* 3A **32**
Harker. *Cumb* 1C **8**
Harkland. *Shet* 3G **101**
Harlosh. *High* 1B **62**
Haroldswick. *Shet* 1H **101**
Harpsdale. *High* 2A **90**
Harraby. *Cumb* 2D **9**
Harrapool. *High* 3F **63**
Harrapul. *High* 3F **63**
Harrietfield. *Per* 1E **41**
Harrington. *Cumb* 4E **7**
Harriston. *Cumb* 3A **8**
Harthill. *N Lan* 3B **32**
Hartmount Holdings. *High* 2E **77**
Hartwood. *N Lan* 4A **32**
Hassendean. *Bord* 3E **23**
Haster. *High* 2C **90**
Hastigrow. *High* 1B **90**
Hatton. *Abers* 2F **71**
Hattoncrook. *Abers* 3D **71**
Hatton of Fintray. *Abers* 4D **71**
Haugh. *E Ayr* 3F **19**
Haugh Head. *Nmbd* 3D **25**
Haugh of Ballechin. *Per* 2E **49**
Haugh of Glass. *Mor* 2F **69**
Haugh of Urr. *Dum* 1D **7**

Kingswells—Longniddry


Kingswells. *Aber* 1D 61
Kingswood. *Per* 4F 49
Kingussie. *High* 1E 57
Kinharrachie. *Abers* 2E 71
Kinhrive. *High* 2D 77
Kinkell Bridge. *Per* 2E 41
Kinknockie. *Abers* 1F 71
Kinkry Hill. *Cumb* 4E 15
Kinloch. *High* 4E 87
(nr. Loch More)
Kinloch. *High* 2D 45
(nr. Lochaline)
Kinloch. *High* 2C 52
(on Rùm)
Kinloch. *Per* 3A 50
Kinlochard. *Stir* 3F 39
Kinlochbervie. *High* 2D 87
Kinlocheil. *High* 4C 54
Kinlochewe. *High* 3D 75
Kinloch Hourn. *High* 1C 54
Kinloch Laggan. *High* 3C 56
Kinlochleven. *High* 1C 46
Kinloch Lodge. *High* 2A 88
Kinlochmoidart. *High* 4A 54
Kinlochmore. *High* 1C 46
Kinloch Rannoch. *Per* 2B 48
Kinlochspelve. *Arg* 1D 37
Kinloid. *High* 3F 53
Kinloss. *Mor* 3B 78
Kinmuck. *Abers* 4D 71
Kinnadie. *Abers* 1E 71
Kinnaird. *Per* 1B 42
Kinneff. *Abers* 4D 61
Kinnelhead. *Dum* 1F 13
Kinnell. *Ang* 2F 51
Kinnernie. *Abers* 1C 60
Kinnesswood. *Per* 3A 42
Kinnordy. *Ang* 2C 50
Kinross. *Per* 3A 42
Kinrossie. *Per* 4A 50
Kintessack. *Mor* 3B 78
Kintillo. *Per* 2A 42
Kintore. *Abers* 4C 70
Kintour. *Arg* 4E 27
Kintra. *Arg* 1A 36
Kintraw. *Arg* 3F 37
Kinveachy. *High* 4A 68
Kippen. *Stir* 4B 40
Kippford. *Dum* 2D 7
Kirbister. *Orkn* 2B 98
(nr. Hobbister)
Kirbister. *Orkn* 1A 98
(nr. Quholm)
Kirbuster. *Orkn* 5H 99
Kirk. *High* 2B 90
Kirkabister. *Shet* 3C 100
(on Bressay)
Kirkabister. *Shet* 1C 100
(on Mainland)
Kirkandrews. *Dum* 3B 6
Kirkandrews-on-Eden. *Cumb* 2C 8
Kirkapol. *Arg* 3F 91
Kirkbampton. *Cumb* 2C 8
Kirkbean. *Dum* 2E 7
Kirkbride. *Cumb* 2B 8
Kirkbuddo. *Ang* 3E 51
Kirkby Thore. *Cumb* 4F 9
**Kirkcaldy**. *Fife* 106 (4B 42)
Kirkcambeck. *Cumb* 1E 9
Kirkcolm. *Dum* 1B 4
Kirkconnel. *Dum* 4C 20
Kirkconnell. *Dum* 1E 7
Kirkcowan. *Dum* 1E 5
Kirkcudbright. *Dum* 2B 6
Kirkfieldbank. *S Lan* 1D 21
Kirkforthar Feus. *Fife* 3B 42
Kirkgunzeon. *Dum* 1D 7
Kirkhill. *Ang* 1F 51
Kirkhill. *High* 1C 66
Kirkhope. *S Lan* 1E 13
Kirkhouse. *Bord* 2C 22
Kirkibost. *High* 4E 63
Kirkinch. *Ang* 3C 50
Kirkinner. *Dum* 2F 5
**Kirkintilloch**. *E Dun* 2E 31
Kirkland. *Cumb* 4F 9
(nr. Penrith)
Kirkland. *Cumb* 3B 8
(nr. Wigton)
Kirkland. *Dum* 4C 20
(nr. Kirkconnel)
Kirkland. *Dum* 2D 13
(nr. Moniaive)
Kirkland Guards. *Cumb* 3A 8
Kirklauchline. *Dum* 2B 4
Kirklinton. *Cumb* 1D 9
Kirkliston. *Edin* 2D 33
Kirkmabreck. *Dum* 2F 5
Kirkmaiden. *Dum* 4C 4
Kirkmichael. *Per* 1F 49
Kirkmichael. *S Ayr* 1E 11
Kirkmuirhill. *S Lan* 1C 20
Kirknewton. *Nmbd* 2C 24
Kirknewton. *W Lot* 3D 33
Kirkney. *Abers* 2A 70
Kirk of Shotts. *N Lan* 3A 32
Kirkoswald. *Cumb* 3E 9
Kirkoswald. *S Ayr* 1D 11
Kirkpatrick. *Dum* 2E 13
Kirkpatrick Durham. *Dum* 4C 12
Kirkpatrick-Fleming. *Dum* 4B 14
Kirkstile. *Dum* 2C 14
Kirkstyle. *High* 5B 98
Kirkton. *Abers* 4B 70
(nr. Alford)
Kirkton. *Abers* 3B 70
(nr. Insch)
Kirkton. *Abers* 1D 71
(nr. Turriff)
Kirkton. *Ang* 4D 51
(nr. Dundee)
Kirkton. *Ang* 3D 51
(nr. Forfar)
Kirkton. *Ang* 3F 59
(nr. Tarfside)
Kirkton. *Dum* 3E 13
Kirkton. *Fife* 1C 42
Kirkton. *High* 4C 84
(nr. Golspie)
Kirkton. *High* 3B 64
(nr. Kyle of Lochalsh)
Kirkton. *High* 1C 64
(nr. Lochcarron)
Kirkton. *Bord* 4E 23
Kirkton. *S Lan* 3E 21
Kirktonhill. *W Dun* 2B 30
Kirkton Manor. *Bord* 2B 22
Kirkton of Airlie. *Ang* 2C 50
Kirkton of Auchterhouse.
*Ang* 4C 50
Kirkton of Bourtie. *Abers* 3D 71
Kirkton of Collace. *Per* 4A 50
Kirkton of Craig. *Ang* 2F 51
Kirkton of Culsalmond.
*Abers* 2B 70
Kirkton of Durris. *Abers* 2C 60
Kirkton of Glenbuchat.
*Abers* 4E 69
Kirkton of Glenisla. *Ang* 1B 50
Kirkton of Kingoldrum.
*Ang* 2C 50
Kirkton of Largo. *Fife* 3D 43
Kirkton of Lethendy. *Per* 3A 50
Kirkton of Logie Buchan.
*Abers* 3E 71
Kirkton of Maryculter.
*Abers* 2D 61
Kirkton of Menmuir. *Ang* 1E 51
Kirkton of Monikie. *Ang* 4E 51
Kirkton of Oyne. *Abers* 3B 70
Kirkton of Rayne. *Abers* 2B 70
Kirkton of Skene. *Abers* 1D 61
Kirktown. *Abers* 3E 81
(nr. Fraserburgh)
Kirktown. *Abers* 4F 81
(nr. Peterhead)
Kirktown of Alvah. *Abers* 3B 80
Kirktown of Auchterless.
*Abers* 1C 70
Kirktown of Deskford. *Mor* 3A 80
Kirktown of Fetteresso.
*Abers* 3D 61
Kirktown of Mortlach. *Mor* 2E 69
Kirktown of Slains. *Abers* 3F 71
Kirkurd. *Bord* 1A 22
Kirkwall. *Orkn* 1C 98
Kirkwall Airport. *Orkn* 2C 98
Kirk Yetholm. *Bord* 3B 24
Kirn. *Arg* 2F 29
Kirriemuir. *Ang* 2C 50
Kirtlebridge. *Dum* 4B 14
Kirtleton. *Dum* 4B 14
Kirtomy. *High* 1C 88
Kishorn. *High* 1B 64
Kittybrewster. *Aber* 1E 61
Knapp. *Per* 4B 50
Knapperfield. *High* 2B 90
Knarsdale. *Nmbd* 2F 9
Knaven. *Abers* 1D 71
Knightswood. *Glas* 3D 31
Knock. *Arg* 4C 44
Knock. *Cumb* 4F 9
Knock. *Mor* 4A 80
Knockally. *High* 1F 85
Knockan. *Arg* 1B 36
Knockan. *High* 2D 83
Knockandhu. *Mor* 3D 69
Knockando. *Mor* 1C 68
Knockarthur. *High* 3C 84
Knockbain. *High* 4D 77
Knockbreck. *High* 3B 72
Knockdee. *High* 1A 90
Knockdolian. *S Ayr* 3C 10
Knockdon. *S Ayr* 4E 19
Knockenbaird. *Abers* 3B 70
Knockenkelly. *N Ayr* 3B 18
Knockentiber. *E Ayr* 2E 19
Knockfarrel. *High* 4C 76
Knockglass. *High* 1F 89
Knockie Lodge. *High* 4B 66
Knockinlaw. *E Ayr* 2F 19
Knockinnon. *High* 4A 90
Knockrome. *Arg* 2F 27
Knockshinnoch. *E Ayr* 4F 19
Knockvennie. *Dum* 4C 12
Knockvologan. *Arg* 2A 36
Knott. *High* 4C 72
Knowe. *Dum* 4E 11
Knowefield. *Cumb* 2D 9
Knowehead. *Dum* 2B 12
Knowes. *E Lot* 2C 34
Knoweside. *S Ayr* 4D 19
Knowes of Elrick. *Abers* 4B 80
Kyleakin. *High* 3A 64
**Kyle of Lochalsh**. *High* 3A 64
Kylerhea. *High* 3A 64
Kylesku. *High* 4D 87
Kyles Lodge. *W Isl* 4D 94
Kylesmorar. *High* 2B 54
Kylestrome. *High* 4D 87


## L


Labost. *W Isl* 2D 96
Lacasaidh. *W Isl* 4E 97
Lacasdail. *W Isl* 3F 97
Lady. *Orkn* 3H 99
Ladybank. *Fife* 2C 42
Ladykirk. *Bord* 1B 24
Ladysford. *Abers* 3E 81
Laga. *High* 1D 45
Lagavulin. *Arg* 1B 16
Lagg. *Arg* 2F 27
Lagg. *N Ayr* 3A 18
Laggan. *Arg* 4C 26
Laggan. *High* 2F 55
(nr. Fort Augustus)
Laggan. *High* 2D 57
(nr. Newtonmore)
Laggan. *Mor* 2E 69
Lagganlia. *High* 1F 57
Lagganulva. *Arg* 3B 44
Laglingarten. *Arg* 3C 38
Laid. *High* 2F 87
Laide. *High* 4A 82
Laigh Fenwick. *E Ayr* 1F 19
Lairg. *High* 3A 84
Lairg Muir. *High* 3A 84
Laithes. *Cumb* 4D 9
Lamancha. *Bord* 4E 33
Lambden. *Bord* 1A 24
Lamberton. *Bord* 4F 35
Lambhill. *Glas* 3D 31
Lambley. *Nmbd* 2F 9
Laminess. *Orkn* 4H 99
Lamington. *High* 2E 77
Lamington. *S Lan* 2E 21
Lamlash. *N Ayr* 2B 18
Lamonby. *Cumb* 4D 9
Lanark. *S Lan* 1D 21
Landerberry. *Abers* 1C 60
Landhallow. *High* 4A 90
Lanercost. *Cumb* 1E 9
Langais. *W Isl* 1H 93
Langal. *High* 1E 45
Langbank. *Ren* 2B 30
Langburnshiels. *Bord* 1E 15
Langdyke. *Fife* 3C 42
Langholm. *Dum* 3C 14
Langleeford. *Nmbd* 3C 24
Langrigg. *Cumb* 3A 8
Langshaw. *Bord* 2E 23
Langwathby. *Cumb* 4E 9
Lanton. *Nmbd* 2C 24
Lanton. *Bord* 3F 23
Laphroaig. *Arg* 1A 16
Larachbeg. *High* 3D 45
Larbert. *Falk* 1A 32
Larel. *High* 2A 90
Largie. *Abers* 2B 70
Largiemore. *Arg* 1D 29
Largoward. *Fife* 3D 43
**Largs**. *N Ayr* 4A 30
Largue. *Abers* 1B 70
Largybeg. *N Ayr* 3B 18
Largymeanoch. *N Ayr* 3B 18
Largymore. *N Ayr* 3B 18
Larkfield. *Inv* 2A 30
**Larkhall**. *S Lan* 4F 31
Lary. *Abers* 1E 59
Lasswade. *Midl* 3F 33
Latheron. *High* 4A 90
Latheronwheel. *High* 4A 90
Lathones. *Fife* 3D 43
Laudale House. *High* 2E 45
Lauder. *Bord* 1E 23
Laurencekirk. *Abers* 4C 60
Laurieston. *Dum* 1B 6
Laurieston. *Falk* 2B 32
Laverhay. *Dum* 2A 14
Laversdale. *Cumb* 1D 9
Law. *S Lan* 4A 32
Lawers. *Per* 4B 48
Laxfirth. *Shet* 1C 100
Laxo. *Shet* 5G 101
Lazonby. *Cumb* 4E 9
Leac a Li. *W Isl* 3F 95
Leachd. *Arg* 4B 38
Leachkin. *High* 1D 67
Leadburn. *Midl* 4E 33
Leaderfoot. *Bord* 2E 23
Leadgate. *Cumb* 3F 9
Leadhills. *S Lan* 4D 21
Lealt. *Arg* 4D 37
Lealt. *High* 3E 73
Leargybreck. *Arg* 2F 27
Leaths. *Dum* 1C 6
Leckfurin. *High* 2C 88
Leckgruinart. *Arg* 3C 26
Leckmelm. *High* 4C 82
Ledaig. *Arg* 4A 46
Ledgowan. *High* 4E 75
Ledmore. *High* 2D 83
Lednabirichen. *High* 4C 84
Lednagullin. *High* 1D 89
Leeans. *Shet* 2B 100
Leebotten. *Shet* 4C 100
Leetown. *Per* 1B 42
Legerwood. *Bord* 1E 23
Leirinmore. *High* 1F 87
Leishmore. *High* 1B 66
Leitfie. *Per* 3B 50
Leith. *Edin* 2E 33
Leitholm. *Bord* 1A 24
Lempitlaw. *Bord* 2A 24
Lenchie. *Abers* 2A 70
Lendalfoot. *S Ayr* 3C 10
Lendrick. *Stir* 3A 40
Lenimore. *N Ayr* 1F 17
Lennel. *Bord* 1B 24
Lennoxtown. *E Dun* 2E 31
Lentran. *High* 1C 66
**Lenzie**. *E Dun* 2E 31
Leochel Cushnie. *Abers* 4A 70
Leogh. *Shet* 1H 99
Lephenstrath. *Arg* 4D 17
Lephin. *High* 1A 62
Lephinchapel. *Arg* 4A 38
Lephinmore. *Arg* 4A 38
Lerwick. *Shet* 2C 100
Lerwick (Tingwall) Airport.
*Shet* 2C 100
Lesbury. *Nmbd* 4F 25
Leslie. *Abers* 3A 70
Leslie. *Fife* 3B 42
Lesmahagow. *S Lan* 2D 21
Lessonhall. *Cumb* 2B 8
Leswalt. *Dum* 1B 4
Letham. *Ang* 3E 51
Letham. *Falk* 1A 32
Letham. *Fife* 2C 42
Lethanhill. *E Ayr* 4F 19
Lethenty. *Abers* 1D 71
Lettan. *Orkn* 3H 99
Letter. *Abers* 4C 70
Letterewe. *High* 2C 74
Letterfearn. *High* 3B 64
Lettermore. *Arg* 3B 44
Letters. *High* 1E 75
Leuchars. *Fife* 1D 43
Leumrabhagh. *W Isl* 1H 95
Levaneap. *Shet* 5G 101
Leven. *Fife* 3C 42
Levencorroch. *N Ayr* 3B 18
Levenhall. *E Lot* 2F 33
Levenwick. *Shet* 4C 100
Leverburgh. *W Isl* 4E 95
Levishie. *High* 4B 66
Lewiston. *High* 3C 66
Leylodge. *Abers* 4C 70
Leys. *Per* 4B 50
Leysmill. *Ang* 3F 51
Lhanbryde. *Mor* 3D 79
Liatrie. *High* 2F 65
Libberton. *S Lan* 1E 21
Liberton. *Edin* 3E 33
Liceasto. *W Isl* 3F 95
Liddle. *Orkn* 4C 98
Lienassie. *High* 3C 64
Liff. *Ang* 4C 50
Lilburn Tower. *Nmbd* 3D 25
Lilliesleaf. *Bord* 3E 23
Lilybank. *Inv* 2B 30
Limekilnburn. *S Lan* 4F 31
Limekilns. *Fife* 1C 32
Limerigg. *Falk* 2A 32
Linburn. *W Lot* 3D 33
Lincluden. *Dum* 4E 13
Lindean. *Bord* 2D 23
Lindores. *Fife* 2B 42
Lingreabhagh. *W Isl* 4E 95
Lingy Close. *Cumb* 2C 8
Linicro. *High* 3C 72
Linklater. *Orkn* 4C 98
Linksness. *Orkn* 1D 98
Linktown. *Fife* 4B 42
Linkwood. *Mor* 3D 79
**Linlithgow**. *W Lot* 2B 32
Linlithgow Bridge. *Falk* 2B 32
Linneraineach. *High* 3C 82
Linshiels. *Nmbd* 4B 24
Linsiadar. *W Isl* 3D 96
Linsidemore. *High* 4A 84
Linstock. *Cumb* 2D 9
Lintlaw. *Bord* 4E 35
Lintmill. *Mor* 3A 80
Linton. *Bord* 3A 24
**Linwood**. *Ren* 3C 30
Lionacleit. *W Isl* 3G 93
Lionacro. *High* 3C 72
Lionacuidhe. *W Isl* 3G 93
Lional. *W Isl* 1G 97
Liquo. *N Lan* 4A 32
Littemill. *Nmbd* 4F 25
Litterty. *Abers* 4C 80
Little Ardo. *Abers* 2D 71
Little Ballinluig. *Per* 2E 49
Little Bampton. *Cumb* 2B 8
Little Blencow. *Cumb* 4D 9
Little Brechin. *Ang* 1E 51
Little Broughton. *Cumb* 4F 7
Little Clifton. *Cumb* 4F 7
Little Creich. *High* 1D 77
Little Crosthwaite. *Cumb* 4B 8
Little Dens. *Abers* 1F 71
Little Dunkeld. *Per* 3F 49
Littleferry. *High* 4D 85
Little Glenshee. *Per* 4E 49
Littlehoughton. *Nmbd* 4F 25
Littlemill. *Abers* 2E 59
Littlemill. *E Ayr* 4F 19
Littlemill. *High* 1A 68
Little Orton. *Cumb* 2C 8
Little Rogart. *High* 3C 84
Little Ryle. *Nmbd* 4D 25
Little Salkeld. *Cumb* 4E 9
Little Scatwell. *High* 4A 76
Littlester. *Shet* 3H 101
Little Torboll. *High* 4C 84
Littletown. *High* 1E 77
Liurbost. *W Isl* 4E 97
**Livingston**. *W Lot* 3C 32
Livingston Village. *W Lot* 3C 32
Loan. *Falk* 2B 32
Loanend. *Nmbd* 4F 35
Loanhead. *Midl* 3E 33
Loaningfoot. *Dum* 2E 7
Loanreoch. *High* 2D 77
Loans. *S Ayr* 2E 19
Lochaber. *Mor* 4B 78
Loch a Charnain. *W Isl* 3H 93
Loch a Ghainmhich. *W Isl* 4D 96
Lochailort. *High* 3A 54
Lochaline. *High* 3D 45
Lochans. *Dum* 2B 4
Locharbriggs. *Dum* 3E 13
Lochardil. *High* 1D 67
Lochassynt Lodge. *High* 1C 82
Lochavich. *Arg* 2A 38
Lochawe. *Arg* 1C 38
Loch Baghasdail. *W Isl* 1C 92
Lochboisdale. *W Isl* 1C 92
Lochbuie. *Arg* 1D 37
Lochcarron. *High* 2B 64
Loch Choire Lodge. *High* 4B 88
Lochdochart House. *Stir* 1F 39
Lochdon. *Arg* 4E 45
Lochearnhead. *Stir* 1A 40
Lochee. *D'dee* 4C 50
Lochend. *High* 2C 66
(nr. Inverness)
Lochend. *High* 1B 90
(nr. Thurso)
Locherben. *Dum* 2E 13
Loch Euphort. *W Isl* 1H 93
Lochfoot. *Dum* 4D 13
Lochgair. *Arg* 4A 38
Lochgarthside. *High* 4C 66
Lochgelly. *Fife* 4A 42
Lochgilphead. *Arg* 1C 28
Lochgoilhead. *Arg* 3C 38
Loch Head. *Dum* 3E 5
Lochhill. *Mor* 3D 79
Lochindorb Lodge. *High* 2A 68
Lochinver. *High* 1B 82
Lochlane. *Per* 1D 41
Loch Lomond. *Arg* 3E 39
Loch Loyal Lodge. *High* 3B 88
Lochluichart. *High* 3A 76
Lochmaben. *Dum* 3F 13
Lochmaddy. *W Isl* 1H 93
Loch nam Madadh. *W Isl* 1H 93
Lochore. *Fife* 4A 42
Lochportain. *W Isl* 5D 94
Lochranza. *N Ayr* 4D 29
Loch Sgioport. *W Isl* 4H 93
Lochside. *Abers* 1F 51
Lochside. *High* 4D 89
(nr. Achentoul)
Lochside. *High* 4F 77
(nr. Nairn)
Lochslin. *High* 1F 77
Lochstack Lodge. *High* 3D 87
Lochton. *Abers* 2C 60
Lochty. *Fife* 3E 43
Lochuisge. *High* 2E 45
Lochussie. *High* 4B 76
Lochwinnoch. *Ren* 4B 30
Lochyside. *High* 4E 55
Lockerbie. *Dum* 3A 14
Lockhills. *Cumb* 3E 9
Logan. *E Ayr* 3A 20
Loganlea. *W Lot* 3B 32
Loggie. *High* 4C 82
Logie. *Ang* 1F 51
Logie. *Fife* 1D 43
Logie. *Mor* 4B 78
Logie Coldstone. *Abers* 1F 59
Logie Pert. *Ang* 1F 51
Logierait. *Per* 2E 49
Lonbain. *High* 4F 73
Londubh. *High* 1B 74
Lone. *High* 3E 87
Lonemore. *High* 1E 77
(nr. Dornoch)
Lonemore. *High* 2A 74
(nr. Gairloch)
Longbar. *N Ayr* 4B 30
Longburgh. *Cumb* 2C 8
Longcroft. *Cumb* 2B 8
Longcroft. *Falk* 2F 31
Longdales. *Cumb* 3E 9
Longfield. *Shet* 5B 100
Longforgan. *Per* 4C 50
Longformacus. *Bord* 4C 34
Longhill. *Abers* 4F 81
Longhope. *Orkn* 3B 98
Longhoughton. *Nmbd* 4F 25
Longlands. *Cumb* 4B 8
Longmanhill. *Abers* 3C 80
Long Marton. *Cumb* 4F 9
Longmorn. *Mor* 4D 79
Longnewton. *Bord* 3E 23
Longniddry. *E Lot* 2A 34

Newbiggin—Ramscraigs


Newbiggin. *Cumb* 4F 9 (nr. Appleby)
Newbiggin. *Cumb* 3E 9 (nr. Cumrew)
Newbiggin. *Cumb* 4D 9 (nr. Penrith)
Newbigging. *Ang* 4D 51 (nr. Monikie)
Newbigging. *Ang* 3B 50 (nr. Newtyle)
Newbigging. *Ang* 4D 51 (nr. Tealing)
Newbigging. *Edin* 2D 33
Newbigging. *S Lan* 1F 21
New Bridge. *Dum* 4E 13
Newbridge. *Edin* 2D 33
Newburgh. *Abers* 3E 71
Newburgh. *Fife* 2B 42
Newby East. *Cumb* 2D 9
New Byth. *Abers* 4D 81
Newby West. *Cumb* 2C 8
Newcastleton. *Bord* 3D 15
New Cowper. *Cumb* 3A 8
Newcraighall. *Edin* 2F 33
New Cumnock. *E Ayr* 4B 20
New Deer. *Abers* 1D 71
New Elgin. *Mor* 3D 79
New Galloway. *Dum* 4B 12
Newham. *Nmbd* 3E 25
Newhaven. *Edin* 2E 33
Newhouse. *N Lan* 3F 31
Newington. *Edin* 2E 33
New Kelso. *High* 1C 64
New Lanark. *S Lan* 1D 21
Newlandrig. *Midl* 3F 33
Newlands. *Cumb* 4C 8
Newlands. *High* 1E 67
Newlands of Geise. *High* 1F 89
Newlands of Tynet. *Mor* 3E 79
New Langholm. *Dum* 3C 14
New Leeds. *Abers* 4E 81
Newlot. *Orkn* 1D 98
New Luce. *Dum* 1C 4
Newmachar. *Abers* 4D 71
Newmains. *N Lan* 4A 32
New Mains of Ury. *Abers* 3D 61
Newmarket. *W Isl* 3F 97
New Mill. *Abers* 1C 70
Newmill. *Mor* 4F 79
Newmill. *Bord* 4D 23
Newmills. *Fife* 1C 32
Newmills. *High* 3D 77
Newmiln. *Per* 4A 50
Newmilns. *E Ayr* 2A 20
Newmore. *High* 4C 76 (nr. Dingwall)
Newmore. *High* 2D 77 (nr. Invergordon)
Newpark. *Fife* 2D 43
New Pitsligo. *Abers* 4D 81
Newport. *High* 1F 85
Newport-on-Tay. *Fife* 1D 43
New Prestwick. *S Ayr* 3E 19
New Rent. *Cumb* 4D 9
New Sauchie. *Clac* 4D 41
Newseat. *Abers* 2C 70
New Shoreston. *Nmbd* 2E 25
Newstead. *Bord* 2E 23
New Stevenston. *N Lan* 4F 31
Newton. *Arg* 4B 38
Newton. *Dum* 4B 14 (nr. Annan)
Newton. *Dum* 2A 14 (nr. Moffat)
Newton. *High* 3E 77 (nr. Cromarty)
Newton. *High* 1E 67 (nr. Inverness)
Newton. *High* 4D 87 (nr. Kylestrome)
Newton. *High* 3C 90 (nr. Wick)
Newton. *Mor* 3C 78
Newton. *Bord* 3F 23
Newton. *Shet* 3B 100
Newton. *S Lan* 3E 31 (nr. Glasgow)
Newton. *S Lan* 2E 21 (nr. Lanark)
Newton. *W Lot* 2C 32
Newtonairds. *Dum* 3D 13
Newton Arlosh. *Cumb* 2B 8
Newtongrange. *Midl* 3F 33
Newtonhill. *Abers* 2E 61
Newtonhill. *High* 1C 66
**Newton Mearns**. *E Ren* 4D 31
**Newtonmore**. *High* 2E 57
Newton of Ardtoe. *High* 4F 53
Newton of Balcanquhal. *Per* 2A 42
Newton of Beltrees. *Ren* 4B 30
Newton of Falkland. *Fife* 3B 42
Newton of Mountblairy. *Abers* 4B 80
Newton of Pitcairns. *Per* 2F 41
Newton-on-the-Moor. *Nmbd* 4E 25
Newton Reigny. *Cumb* 4D 9
Newton Rigg. *Cumb* 4D 9
Newton Stewart. *Dum* 1F 5
Newton upon Ayr. *S Ayr* 3E 19
New Town. *E Lot* 2A 34
Newtown. *Abers* 3C 80
Newtown. *Cumb* 3F 7 (nr. Aspatria)
Newtown. *Cumb* 1E 9 (nr. Brampton)
Newtown. *Cumb* 4E 9 (nr. Penrith)
Newtown. *Falk* 1B 32
Newtown. *High* 1A 56
Newtown. *Nmbd* 3D 25
Newtown. *Shet* 3G 101
Newtown St Boswells. *Bord* 2E 23
Newtyle. *Ang* 3B 50
New Winton. *E Lot* 2A 34
Niddrie. *Edin* 2F 33
Niddry. *W Lot* 2C 32
Nigg. *Aber* 1E 61
Nigg. *High* 2F 77
Nigg Ferry. *High* 3E 77
Ninemile Bar. *Dum* 4D 13
Nine Mile Burn. *Midl* 4D 33
Nisbet. *Bord* 3F 23
Nisbet Hill. *Bord* 4D 35
Nitshill. *Glas* 3D 31
Noness. *Shet* 4C 100
Nonikiln. *High* 2D 77
Nook. *Cumb* 4D 15
Noranside. *Ang* 1D 51
Norby. *Shet* 1A 100
Norham. *Nmbd* 1C 24
North Balfern. *Dum* 2F 5
North Ballachulish. *High* 1B 46
North Berwick. *E Lot* 1B 34
North Charlton. *Nmbd* 3E 25
North Collafirth. *Shet* 3F 101
North Commonty. *Abers* 1D 71
North Craigo. *Ang* 1F 51
North Dronley. *Ang* 4C 50
Northdyke. *Orkn* 1A 98
North Erradale. *High* 1A 74
North Fearns. *High* 2E 63
North Feorline. *N Ayr* 3A 18
Northfield. *Aber* 1D 61
North Gluss. *Shet* 4F 101
North Hazelrigg. *Nmbd* 2D 25
North Kessock. *High* 1D 67
North Middleton. *Midl* 4F 33
North Middleton. *Nmbd* 3D 25
Northmuir. *Ang* 2C 50
North Murie. *Per* 1B 42
North Ness. *Orkn* 3B 98
North Port. *Arg* 1B 38
North Queensferry. *Fife* 1D 33
North Roe. *Shet* 3F 101
North Ronaldsay Airport. *Orkn* 2H 99
North Row. *Cumb* 4B 8
North Sannox. *N Ayr* 1B 18
North Shian. *Arg* 3A 46
North Side. *Cumb* 4F 7
North Sunderland. *Nmbd* 2F 25
North Town. *Shet* 5B 100
Northtown. *Orkn* 3C 98
Northwall. *Orkn* 3H 99
North Water Bridge. *Ang* 1F 51
North Watten. *High* 2B 90
Norwick. *Shet* 1H 101
Noss. *Shet* 5B 100
Nostie. *High* 3B 64
Nunclose. *Cumb* 3D 9
Nunnerie. *S Lan* 4E 21
Nybster. *High* 1C 90


## O


Oakbank. *Arg* 4E 45
Oakbank. *W Lot* 3C 32
Oakley. *Fife* 1C 32
Oakshaw Ford. *Cumb* 4E 15
Oape. *High* 3F 83
Oathlaw. *Ang* 2D 51
**Oban**. *Arg* 106 (1F 37)
Oban. *W Isl* 2F 95
Obsdale. *High* 3D 77
Ochiltree. *E Ayr* 3A 20
Ochtermuthill. *Per* 2D 41
Ochtertyre. *Per* 1D 41
Ockle. *High* 4E 53
Octofad. *Arg* 4C 26
Octomore. *Arg* 4C 26
Oddsta. *Shet* 2H 101
Odie. *Orkn* 5H 99
Okraquoy. *Shet* 3C 100
Old Aberdeen. *Aber* 1E 61
Oldany. *High* 4C 86
Old Bewick. *Nmbd* 3D 25
Old Blair. *Per* 1D 49
Old Bridge of Tilt. *Per* 1D 49
Old Bridge of Urr. *Dum* 1C 6
Old Dailly. *S Ayr* 2D 11
Old Deer. *Abers* 1E 71
Old Graitney. *Dum* 1C 8
Oldhall. *High* 2B 90
Oldhamstocks. *E Lot* 2D 35
Old Kilpatrick. *W Dun* 2C 30
Old Kinnernie. *Abers* 1C 60
Oldmeldrum. *Abers* 3D 71
Old Monkland. *N Lan* 3F 31
Old Pentland. *Midl* 3E 33
Old Philpstoun. *W Lot* 2C 32
Old Rayne. *Abers* 3B 70
Old Scone. *Per* 1A 42
Oldshore Beg. *High* 2C 86
Oldshoremore. *High* 2D 87
Old Town. *Cumb* 3D 9
Oldtown. *High* 1C 76
Oldwall. *Cumb* 1D 9
Old Westhall. *Abers* 3B 70
Oldwhat. *Abers* 4D 81
Olgrinmore. *High* 2F 89
Ollaberry. *Shet* 3F 101
Olrig. *High* 1A 90
Omunsgarth. *Shet* 2B 100
Onich. *High* 1B 46
Onthank. *E Ayr* 2F 19
Opinan. *High* 2A 74 (nr. Gairloch)
Opinan. *High* 4A 82 (nr. Laide)
Orasaigh. *W Isl* 1H 95
Orbost. *High* 1B 62
Ord. *High* 4F 63
Ordale. *Shet* 1H 101
Ordhead. *Abers* 4B 70
Ordie. *Abers* 1F 59
Ordiquish. *Mor* 4E 79
Orgil. *Orkn* 2A 98
Ormacleit. *W Isl* 4G 93
Ormathwaite. *Cumb* 4B 8
Ormiscaig. *High* 1B 74
Ormiston. *E Lot* 3A 34
Ormsaigbeg. *High* 1B 44
Ormsaigmore. *High* 1B 44
Ormsary. *Arg* 2B 28
Orphir. *Orkn* 2B 98
Orthwaite. *Cumb* 4B 8
Orton. *Mor* 4E 79
Osclay. *High* 4B 90
Ose. *High* 1C 62
Oskaig. *High* 2E 63
Oskamull. *Arg* 4B 44
Osmondwall. *Orkn* 4B 98
Osnaburgh. *Fife* 2D 43
Ospisdale. *High* 1E 77
Otter Ferry. *Arg* 1D 29
Otterswick. *Shet* 3H 101
Oughterby. *Cumb* 2B 8
Oughterside. *Cumb* 3A 8
Oulton. *Cumb* 2B 8
Ousby. *Cumb* 4F 9
Ousdale. *High* 2F 85
Outertown. *Orkn* 1A 98
Overbister. *Orkn* 3H 99
Over Finlarg. *Ang* 3D 51
Overscaig. *High* 1F 83
Overton. *Aber* 4D 71
Overton. *High* 4B 90
Overtown. *N Lan* 4A 32
Oxgangs. *Edin* 3E 33
Oxnam. *Bord* 4A 24
Oxton. *Bord* 4A 34
Oykel Bridge. *High* 3E 83
Oyne. *Abers* 3B 70


## P


Pabail Iarach. *W Isl* 3G 97
Pabail Uarach. *W Isl* 3G 97
Padanaram. *Ang* 2D 51
Paddockhole. *Dum* 3B 14
Paibeil. *W Isl* 1G 93 (on North Uist)
Paibeil. *W Isl* 3E 95 (on Taransay)
Paiblesgearraidh. *W Isl* 1G 93
Pairc Shiaboist. *W Isl* 2D 96
**Paisley**. *Ren* 107 (3C 30)
Palgowan. *Dum* 3E 11
Palnackie. *Dum* 2D 7
Palnure. *Dum* 1F 5
Panbride. *Ang* 4E 51
Pannanich. *Abers* 2E 59
Papa Stour Airport. *Shet* 1A 100
Papa Westray Airport. *Orkn* 2F 99
Papcastle. *Cumb* 4A 8
Papigoe. *High* 2C 90
Papil. *Shet* 3B 100
Papple. *E Lot* 2B 34
Pardshaw. *Cumb* 4F 7
Park. *Abers* 2C 60
Park. *Arg* 3A 46
Park. *Dum* 2E 13
Parkburn. *Abers* 2C 70
Parkgate. *Cumb* 3B 8
Parkgate. *Dum* 3F 13
Parkhall. *W Dun* 2C 30
Parkhead. *Cumb* 3C 8
Parkhead. *Glas* 3E 31
Parkneuk. *Abers* 4C 60
Parkside. *N Lan* 4A 32
Park Village. *Nmbd* 1F 9
Parsonby. *Cumb* 4A 8
Partick. *Glas* 3D 31
Parton. *Cumb* 2B 8
Parton. *Dum* 4B 12
Pathhead. *Abers* 1F 51
Pathhead. *E Ayr* 4B 20
Pathhead. *Fife* 4B 42
Pathhead. *Midl* 3F 33
Path of Condie. *Per* 2F 41
Pathstruie. *Per* 2F 41
Patna. *E Ayr* 4F 19
Pattiesmuir. *Fife* 1C 32
Pawston. *Nmbd* 2B 24
Paxton. *Bord* 4F 35
Pearsie. *Ang* 2C 50
Peaston. *E Lot* 3A 34
Peastonbank. *E Lot* 3A 34
Peathill. *Abers* 3E 81
Peat Inn. *Fife* 3D 43
Peaton. *Arg* 1A 30
Peebles. *Bord* 1B 22
Peel. *Bord* 2D 23
Peinchorran. *High* 2E 63
Peinlich. *High* 4D 73
Pelutho. *Cumb* 3A 8
Pencaitland. *E Lot* 3A 34
**Penicuik**. *Midl* 3E 33
Penifiler. *High* 1D 63
Peninver. *Arg* 3E 17
Penkill. *S Ayr* 2D 11
Pennan. *Abers* 3D 81
Pennyghael. *Arg* 1C 36
Pennyvenie. *E Ayr* 1F 11
Penpont. *Dum* 2D 13
**Penrith**. *Cumb* 4E 9
Penruddock. *Cumb* 4D 9
Penston. *E Lot* 2A 34
Perceton. *N Ayr* 1E 19
Percyhorner. *Abers* 3E 81
**Perth**. *Per* 107 (1A 42)
Peterburn. *High* 1A 74
Peterculter. *Aber* 1D 61
**Peterhead**. *Abers* 1F 71
Petertown. *Orkn* 2B 98
Pettinain. *S Lan* 1E 21
Pettycur. *Fife* 1E 33
Philiphaugh. *Bord* 3D 23
Philpstoun. *W Lot* 2C 32
Pickletillem. *Fife* 1D 43
Pierowall. *Orkn* 3F 99
Pilton. *Edin* 2E 33
Pinkerton. *E Lot* 2D 35
Pinmore. *S Ayr* 2D 11
Pinwherry. *S Ayr* 3C 10
Piperhill. *High* 4F 77
Pirnmill. *N Ayr* 1F 17
Pisgah. *Stir* 3C 40
Pitagowan. *Per* 1D 49
Pitcairn. *Per* 2D 49
Pitcairngreen. *Per* 1F 41
Pitcalnie. *High* 2F 77
Pitcaple. *Abers* 3C 70
Pitcox. *E Lot* 2C 34
Pitcur. *Per* 4B 50
Pitfichie. *Abers* 4B 70
Pitgrudy. *High* 4C 84
Pitkennedy. *Ang* 2E 51
Pitlessie. *Fife* 3C 42
Pitlochry. *Per* 2E 49
Pitmachie. *Abers* 3B 70
Pitmaduthy. *High* 2E 77
Pitmedden. *Abers* 3D 71
Pitnacree. *Per* 2E 49
Pitroddie. *Per* 1B 42
Pitscottie. *Fife* 2D 43
Pittentrail. *High* 3C 84
Pittenweem. *Fife* 3E 43
Pittulie. *Abers* 3E 81
Pitversie. *Per* 2A 42
Plaidy. *Abers* 4C 80
Plains. *N Lan* 3F 31
Plean. *Stir* 1A 32
Plenmeller. *Nmbd* 1F 9
Plockton. *High* 2B 64
Plocrapol. *W Isl* 3F 95
Plumbland. *Cumb* 4A 8
Plumpton. *Cumb* 4D 9
Plumpton Foot. *Cumb* 4D 9
Plumpton Head. *Cumb* 4E 9
Polbae. *Dum* 4D 11
Polbain. *High* 3B 82
Polbeth. *W Lot* 3C 32
Polchar. *High* 1F 57
Poles. *High* 4C 84
Polglass. *High* 3B 82
Polio. *High* 2E 77
Polla. *High* 2E 87
Polloch. *High* 1E 45
Pollok. *Glas* 3D 31
Pollokshaws. *Glas* 3D 31
Pollokshields. *Glas* 3D 31
Polmaily. *High* 2B 66
**Polmont**. *Falk* 2B 32
Polnessan. *E Ayr* 4F 19
Polnish. *High* 3A 54
Polskeoch. *Dum* 1B 12
Polton. *Midl* 3E 33
Polwarth. *Bord* 4D 35
Ponton. *Shet* 1B 100
Poolewe. *High* 1B 74
Pooley Bridge. *Cumb* 4D 9
Pool o' Muckhart. *Clac* 3F 41
Porin. *High* 4A 76
Portachoillan. *Arg* 4B 28
Port Adhair Bheinn na Faoghla. *W Isl* 2G 93
Port Adhair Thirlodh. *Arg* 3F 91
Port Ann. *Arg* 1D 29
Port Appin. *Arg* 3A 46
Port Asgaig. *Arg* 3E 27
Port Askaig. *Arg* 3E 27
Portavadie. *Arg* 3D 29
Port Bannatyne. *Arg* 3E 29
Port Carlisle. *Cumb* 1B 8
Port Charlotte. *Arg* 4C 26
Port Driseach. *Arg* 2D 29
Port Dundas. *Glas* 3D 31
Port Ellen. *Arg* 1A 16
Port Elphinstone. *Abers* 3C 70
Portencalzie. *Dum* 4B 10
Portencross. *N Ayr* 1C 18
Port Erroll. *Abers* 2F 71
Portessie. *Mor* 3F 79
**Port Glasgow**. *Inv* 2B 30
Portgordon. *Mor* 3E 79
Portgower. *High* 2F 85
Port Henderson. *High* 2A 74
Portincaple. *Arg* 4D 39
Portinnisherrich. *Arg* 2A 38
Portknockie. *Mor* 3F 79
Port Lamont. *Arg* 2E 29
Portlethen. *Abers* 2E 61
Portlethen Village. *Abers* 2E 61
Portling. *Dum* 2D 7
Port Logan. *Dum* 3B 4
Portmahomack. *High* 1A 78
Port Mholair. *W Isl* 3G 97
Port Mor. *High* 4D 53
Portnacroish. *Arg* 3A 46
Portnahaven. *Arg* 4B 26
Portnalong. *High* 2C 62
Portnaluchaig. *High* 3F 53
Portnancon. *High* 1F 87
Port Nan Giuran. *W Isl* 3G 97
Port nan Long. *W Isl* 5C 94
Port Nis. *W Isl* 1G 97
Portobello. *Edin* 2F 33
Port of Menteith. *Stir* 3A 40
Portormin. *High* 4A 90
Portpatrick. *Dum* 2B 4
Port Ramsay. *Arg* 3F 45
Portree. *High* 1D 63
Port Righ. *High* 1D 63
Port Seton. *E Lot* 2A 34
Portskerra. *High* 1D 89
Portsonachan. *Arg* 1B 38
Portsoy. *Abers* 3A 80
Porttannachy. *Mor* 3E 79
Portuairk. *High* 1B 44
Port Wemyss. *Arg* 4B 26
Port William. *Dum* 3E 5
Potarch. *Abers* 2B 60
Potterton. *Abers* 4E 71
Poundland. *S Ayr* 3C 10
Powburn. *Nmbd* 4D 25
Powfoot. *Dum* 1A 8
Powmill. *Per* 4F 41
Prendwick. *Nmbd* 4D 25
Pressen. *Nmbd* 2B 24
Preston. *E Lot* 2B 34 (nr. East Linton)
Preston. *E Lot* 2F 33 (nr. Prestonpans)
Preston. *Nmbd* 3E 25
Preston. *Bord* 4D 35
Prestonmill. *Dum* 2E 7
Prestonpans. *E Lot* 2F 33
**Prestwick**. *S Ayr* 3E 19
Priesthill. *Glas* 3D 31
Priestland. *E Ayr* 2A 20
Primsidemill. *Bord* 3B 24
Prior Muir. *Fife* 2E 43
Prospect. *Cumb* 3A 8
Provanmill. *Glas* 3E 31
Pulpit Hill. *Arg* 1F 37
Pumpherston. *W Lot* 3C 32


## Q


Quarrier's Village. *Inv* 3B 30
Quarrywood. *Mor* 3C 78
Quartalehouse. *Abers* 1E 71
Quarter. *N Ayr* 3F 29
Quarter. *S Lan* 4F 31
**Queensferry Crossing**. *Edin* 2D 33
Queenzieburn. *N Lan* 2E 31
Quendale. *Shet* 5B 100
Quholm. *Orkn* 1A 98
Quilquox. *Abers* 2E 71
Quindry. *Orkn* 3C 98
Quothquan. *S Lan* 2E 21
Quoyloo. *Orkn* 1A 98
Quoyness. *Orkn* 2A 98
Quoys. *Shet* 5G 101 (on Mainland)
Quoys. *Shet* 1H 101 (on Unst)


## R


Raby. *Cumb* 2A 8
Rachan Mill. *Bord* 2A 22
Racks. *Dum* 4F 13
Rackwick. *Orkn* 3A 98 (on Hoy)
Rackwick. *Orkn* 3F 99 (on Westray)
Radernie. *Fife* 3D 43
Rafford. *Mor* 4B 78
Raggra. *High* 3C 90
Raigbeg. *High* 3F 67
Raise. *Cumb* 3F 9
Rait. *Per* 1B 42
Ralia. *High* 2E 57
Ramasaig. *High* 1A 62
Ramnageo. *Shet* 1H 101
Ramsburn. *Mor* 4A 80
Ramscraigs. *High* 1F 85

Stainburn—Voe


Stainburn. *Cumb* 4F **7**
Stainton. *Cumb* 2C **8**
(nr. Carlisle)
Stainton. *Cumb* 4D **9**
(nr. Penrith)
Stair. *E Ayr* 3F **19**
Stairhaven. *Dum* 2D **5**
Stamford. *Nmbd* 4F **25**
Stamperland. *E Ren* 4D **31**
Stand. *N Lan* 3F **31**
Standburn. *Falk* 2B **32**
Standingstone. *Cumb* 3B **8**
Stane. *N Lan* 4A **32**
Stanecastle. *N Ayr* 2E **19**
Stanhope. *Bord* 3A **22**
Stanley. *Per* 4A **50**
Stannersburn. *Nmbd* 3F **15**
Stanydale. *Shet* 1A **100**
Staoinebrig. *W Isl* 4G **93**
Stapleton. *Cumb* 4E **15**
Star. *Fife* 3C **42**
Staxigoe. *High* 2C **90**
Steelend. *Fife* 4F **41**
Steele Road. *Bord* 2E **15**
Stein. *High* 4B **72**
Steinmanhill. *Abers* 1C **70**
Stemster. *High* 1A **90**
(nr. Halkirk)
Stemster. *High* 1F **89**
(nr. Westfield)
Stenhouse. *Edin* 2E **33**
**Stenhousemuir**. *Falk* 1A **32**
Stenscholl. *High* 3D **73**
Stenso. *Orkn* 5E **99**
Stenton. *E Lot* 2C **34**
Steòrnabhagh. *W Isl* 3F **97**
Stepford. *Dum* 3D **13**
Stepps. *N Lan* 3E **31**
**Stevenston**. *N Ayr* 1D **19**
Stewarton. *Arg* 4D **17**
Stewarton. *E Ayr* 1F **19**
Stichill. *Bord* 2A **24**
Stirling. *Abers* 1F **71**
**Stirling**. *Stir* **107** (4C **40**)
Stittenham. *High* 2D **77**
Stobo. *Bord* 2A **22**
Stobo Castle. *Bord* 2A **22**
Stobs Castle. *Bord* 1E **15**
Stockdalewath. *Cumb* 3C **8**
Stoer. *High* 1B **82**
Stonebyres Holdings.
*S Lan* 1D **21**
Stonefield. *Arg* 4A **46**
Stonefield. *S Lan* 4E **31**
**Stonehaven**. *Abers* 3D **61**
Stonehouse. *Nmbd* 2F **9**
Stonehouse. *S Lan* 1C **20**
Stoneyburn. *W Lot* 3B **32**
Stoneykirk. *Dum* 2B **4**
Stoneywood. *Aber* 4D **71**
Stonybreck. *Shet* 1H **99**
Stormontfield. *Per* 1A **42**
Stornoway. *W Isl* 3F **97**
Stornoway Airport. *W Isl* 3F **97**
Stotfield. *Mor* 2D **79**
Stoul. *High* 2A **54**
Stove. *Orkn* 4H **99**
Stove. *Shet* 4C **100**
Stow. *Bord* 1D **23**
Straad. *Arg* 3E **29**
Strachan. *Abers* 2B **60**
Straid. *S Ayr* 2C **10**
Straiton. *Midl* 3E **33**
Straiton. *S Ayr* 1E **11**
Straloch. *Per* 1F **49**
**Stranraer**. *Dum* 1B **4**
Strath. *High* 2A **74**
(nr. Gairloch)
Strath. *High* 2B **90**
(nr. Wick)
Strathan. *High* 2C **54**
(nr. Fort William)
Strathan. *High* 1B **82**
(nr. Lochinver)
Strathan. *High* 1A **88**
(nr. Tongue)
Strathan Skerray. *High* 1B **88**
Strathaven. *S Lan* 1C **20**
Strathblane. *Stir* 2D **31**
Strathcanaird. *High* 3C **82**
Strathcarron. *High* 1C **64**
Strathcoil. *Arg* 4D **45**
Strathdon. *Abers* 4E **69**
Strathkinness. *Fife* 2D **43**
Strathmashie House. *High* 2C **56**
Strathmiglo. *Fife* 2B **42**
Strathmore Lodge. *High* 3A **90**
Strathpeffer. *High* 4B **76**
Strathrannoch. *High* 2A **76**
Strathtay. *Per* 2E **49**
Strathvaich Lodge. *High* 2A **76**
Strathwhillan. *N Ayr* 2B **18**
Strathy. *High* 2D **77**
(nr. Invergordon)
Strathy. *High* 1D **89**
(nr. Melvich)
Strathyre. *Stir* 2A **40**
Stravithie. *Fife* 2E **43**
Strichen. *Abers* 4E **81**
Stroanfreggan. *Dum* 2B **12**
Stromeferry. *High* 2B **64**
Stromemore. *High* 2B **64**
Stromness. *Orkn* 2A **98**
Stronachie. *Per* 3F **41**
Stronachlachar. *Stir* 2F **39**
Stronchreggan. *High* 4D **55**
Strone. *Arg* 1F **29**
Strone. *High* 3C **66**
(nr. Drumnadrochit)
Strone. *High* 1E **57**
(nr. Kingussie)
Stronenaba. *High* 3F **55**
Stronganess. *Shet* 1H **101**
Stronmilchan. *Arg* 1C **38**
Stronsay Airport. *Orkn* 5H **99**
Strontian. *High* 1F **45**
Struan. *High* 2C **62**
Struan. *Per* 1D **49**
Struanmore. *High* 2C **62**
Strutherhill. *S Lan* 4F **31**
Struy. *High* 2B **66**
Stuartfield. *Abers* 1E **71**
Suainebost. *W Isl* 1G **97**
Suardail. *W Isl* 3F **97**
Succoth. *Abers* 2F **69**
Succoth. *Arg* 3D **39**
Suisnish. *High* 2E **63**
Sulaisiadar. *W Isl* 3G **97**
Sùlaisiadar Mòr. *High* 1D **63**
Sullom. *Shet* 4F **101**
Sumburgh. *Shet* 5C **100**
Sumburgh Airport. *Shet* 5B **100**
Summerhill. *Aber* 1E **61**
Sunderland. *Cumb* 4A **8**
Sunnylaw. *Stir* 4C **40**
Sutors of Cromarty. *High* 3F **77**
Swanbister. *Orkn* 2B **98**
Swarister. *Shet* 3H **101**
Swarland. *Nmbd* 4E **25**
Swiney. *High* 4B **90**
Swinhill. *S Lan* 1C **20**
Swinhoe. *Nmbd* 3F **25**
Swinister. *Shet* 3F **101**
Swinside Hall. *Bord* 4A **24**
Swinton. *Bord* 1B **24**
Swordale. *High* 3C **76**
Swordly. *High* 1C **88**
Symbister. *Shet* 5H **101**
Symington. *S Ayr* 2E **19**
Symington. *S Lan* 2E **21**
Syre. *High* 3B **88**

## T

Tabost. *W Isl* 1H **95**
(nr. Cearsiadar)
Tabost. *W Isl* 1G **97**
(nr. Suainebost)
Tacleit. *W Isl* 3C **96**
Taigh a Ghearraidh. *W Isl* 5B **94**
Taigh Bhuirgh. *W Isl* 3E **95**
Tain. *High* 1E **77**
(nr. Invergordon)
Tain. *High* 1B **90**
(nr. Thurso)
Tairbeart. *W Isl* 3F **95**
Talisker. *High* 2C **62**
Talkin. *Cumb* 2E **9**
Talladale. *High* 2C **74**
Talla Linnfoots. *Bord* 3A **22**
Tallaminnock. *S Ayr* 2E **11**
Tallentire. *Cumb* 4A **8**
Talmine. *High* 1A **88**
Tandlehill. *Ren* 3C **30**
Tangasdal. *W Isl* 2B **92**
Tangwick. *Shet* 4E **101**
Tankerness. *Orkn* 2D **98**
Tannach. *High* 3C **90**
Tannadice. *Ang* 2D **51**
Tannochside. *N Lan* 3F **31**
Taobh a Chaolais. *W Isl* 1C **92**
Taobh a Deas Loch Aineort.
*W Isl* 5G **93**
Taobh a Ghlinne. *W Isl* 1H **95**
Taobh a Tuath Loch Aineort.
*W Isl* 5G **93**
Tarbert. *Arg* 1A **28**
(on Jura)
Tarbert. *Arg* 3C **28**
(on Kintyre)
Tarbert. *W Isl* 3F **95**
Tarbet. *Arg* 3E **39**
Tarbet. *High* 2A **54**
(nr. Mallaig)
Tarbet. *High* 3C **86**
(nr. Scourie)
Tarbolton. *S Ayr* 3F **19**
Tarbrax. *S Lan* 4C **32**
Tarfside. *Ang* 4F **59**
Tarland. *Abers* 1F **59**
Tarlogie. *High* 1E **77**
Tarns. *Cumb* 3A **8**
Tarrel. *High* 1F **77**
Tarsappie. *Per* 1A **42**
Tarscabhaig. *High* 1E **53**
Tarskavaig. *High* 1E **53**
Tarves. *Abers* 2D **71**
Tarvie. *High* 4B **76**
Tavool House. *Arg* 1B **36**
Tayinloan. *Arg* 1D **17**
Taynish. *Arg* 1B **28**
Taynuilt. *Arg* 4B **46**
Tayport. *Fife* 1D **43**
**Tay Road Bridge**.
*D'dee* 1D **43**
Tayvallich. *Arg* 1B **28**
Tealing. *Ang* 4D **51**
Teangue. *High* 1F **53**
Teanna Mhachair.
*W Isl* 1G **93**
Tempar. *Per* 2B **48**
Templand. *Dum* 3F **13**
Temple. *Glas* 3D **31**
Temple. *Midl* 4F **33**
Templehall. *Fife* 4B **42**
Temple Sowerby.
*Cumb* 4F **9**
Tenandry. *Per* 1E **49**
Tenga. *Arg* 3C **44**
Terregles. *Dum* 4E **13**
Teviothead. *Bord* 1D **15**
Tewel. *Abers* 3D **61**
Thackthwaite. *Cumb* 4D **9**
Thankerton. *S Lan* 2E **21**
Thethwaite. *Cumb* 3C **8**
Thirlestane. *Bord* 1E **23**
Thomas Close.
*Cumb* 3D **9**
Thomastown. *Abers* 1C **70**
Thomshill. *Mor* 4D **79**
Thornby. *Cumb* 2B **8**
Thornhill. *Dum* 2D **13**
Thornhill. *Stir* 4B **40**
Thornington. *Nmbd* 2B **24**
Thornliebank. *E Ren* 3D **31**
Thornroan. *Abers* 2D **71**
Thornthwaite. *Cumb* 4B **8**
Thornton. *Ang* 3C **50**
Thornton. *Fife* 4B **42**
Thornton. *Nmbd* 1C **24**
Thorntonhall. *S Lan* 4D **31**
Thorntonloch. *E Lot* 2D **35**
Thrashbush. *N Lan* 3F **31**
Threapland. *Cumb* 4A **8**
Threlkeld. *Cumb* 4C **8**
Throsk. *Stir* 4D **41**
Throughgate. *Dum* 3D **13**
Thrumster. *High* 3C **90**
Thrunton. *Nmbd* 4D **25**
Thundergay. *N Ayr* 1F **17**
Thursby. *Cumb* 2C **8**
**Thurso**. *High* 1A **90**
Thurso East. *High* 1A **90**
Thurstonfield. *Cumb* 2C **8**
Tibbermore. *Per* 1F **41**
Tifty. *Abers* 1C **70**
Tigerton. *Ang* 1E **51**
Tighnabruaich. *Arg* 2D **29**
Tillathrowie. *Abers* 2F **69**
Tillery. *Abers* 3E **71**
Tillicoultry. *Clac* 4E **41**
Tillybirloch. *Abers* 1B **60**
Tillyfourie. *Abers* 4B **70**
Timsgearraidh. *W Isl* 3B **96**
Tindale. *Cumb* 2F **9**
Tingwall. *Orkn* 5F **99**
Tinwald. *Dum* 3F **13**
Tipperty. *Abers* 3E **71**
Tiree Airport. *Arg* 3F **91**
Tirinie. *Per* 1D **49**
Tiroran. *Arg* 1B **36**
Tirril. *Cumb* 4E **9**
Tirryside. *High* 2A **84**
Titlington. *Nmbd* 4D **25**
Toab. *Orkn* 2D **98**
Toab. *Shet* 5B **100**
Tobermory. *Arg* 2C **44**
Toberonochy. *Arg* 3E **37**
Tobha Beag. *W Isl* 4G **93**
Tobha-Beag. *W Isl* 5D **94**
Tobha Mor. *W Isl* 4G **93**
Tobhtarol. *W Isl* 3C **96**
Tobson. *W Isl* 3C **96**
Tocabhaig. *High* 4F **63**
Tocher. *Abers* 2B **70**
Todhills. *Cumb* 1C **8**
Tofts. *High* 1C **90**
Tokavaig. *High* 4F **63**
Tolastadh a Chaolais.
*W Isl* 3C **96**
Tollie. *High* 4C **76**
Tollie Farm. *High* 2B **74**
Tolm. *W Isl* 3F **97**
Tolstadh bho Thuath.
*W Isl* 2G **97**
Tomachlaggan. *Mor* 3C **68**
Tomaknock. *Per* 1D **41**
Tomatin. *High* 3F **67**
Tombuidhe. *Arg* 3B **38**
Tomdoun. *High* 1E **55**
Tomich. *High* 3A **66**
(nr. Cannich)
Tomich. *High* 2E **77**
(nr. Invergordon)
Tomich. *High* 3B **84**
(nr. Lairg)
Tomintoul. *Mor* 4C **68**
Tomnavoulin. *Mor* 3D **69**
Tomsléibhe. *Arg* 4D **45**
Tongland. *Dum* 2B **6**
Tongue. *High* 2A **88**
Torbeg. *N Ayr* 3F **17**
Torbothie. *N Lan* 4A **32**
Tore. *High* 4D **77**
Torgyle. *High* 4A **66**
Torinturk. *Arg* 3C **28**
Torlum. *W Isl* 2G **93**
Torlundy. *High* 4E **55**
Tormitchell. *S Ayr* 2D **11**
Tormore. *High* 1F **53**
Tormore. *N Ayr* 2F **17**
Tornagrain. *High* 1E **67**
Tornaveen. *Abers* 1B **60**
Torness. *High* 3C **66**
Torpenhow. *Cumb* 4B **8**
Torphichen. *W Lot* 2B **32**
Torphins. *Abers* 1B **60**
Torra. *Arg* 4D **27**
Torran. *High* 1E **63**
Torrance. *E Dun* 2E **31**
Torrans. *Arg* 1B **36**
Torranyard. *N Ayr* 1E **19**
Torridon. *High* 4C **74**
Torrin. *High* 3E **63**
Torrisdale. *Arg* 2E **17**
Torrisdale. *High* 1B **88**
Torrish. *High* 2E **85**
Torroble. *High* 3A **84**
Torroy. *High* 4A **84**
Torry. *Aber* 1E **61**
Torryburn. *Fife* 1C **32**
Torthorwald. *Dum* 4F **13**
Torvaig. *High* 1D **63**
Torwood. *Falk* 1A **32**
Toscaig. *High* 2A **64**
Totaig. *High* 4A **72**
Totardor. *High* 2C **62**
Tote. *High* 1D **63**
Totegan. *High* 1D **89**
Totronald. *Arg* 2G **91**
Totscore. *High* 3C **72**
Toulvaddie. *High* 1F **77**
Toward. *Arg* 3F **29**
Towie. *Abers* 4F **69**
Towiemore. *Mor* 1E **69**
Town End. *Cumb* 4F **9**
Townend. *W Dun* 2C **30**
Towngate. *Cumb* 3E **9**
Townhead. *Cumb* 4E **9**
(nr. Lazonby)
Townhead. *Cumb* 4F **7**
(nr. Maryport)
Townhead. *Cumb* 4F **9**
(nr. Ousby)
Townhead. *Dum* 3B **6**
Townhead of Greenlaw.
*Dum* 1C **6**
Townhill. *Fife* 1D **33**
Town Yetholm. *Bord* 3B **24**
Trabboch. *E Ayr* 3F **19**
Tradespark. *High* 4F **77**
Tradespark. *Orkn* 2C **98**
Tranent. *E Lot* 2A **34**
Trantlebeg. *High* 2D **89**
Trantlemore. *High* 2D **89**
Traquair. *Bord* 2C **22**
Treaslane. *High* 4C **72**
Tressady. *High* 3B **84**
Tressait. *Per* 1D **49**
Tresta. *Shet* 2H **101**
(on Fetlar)
Tresta. *Shet* 1B **100**
(on Mainland)
Trinafour. *Per* 1C **48**
Trinity. *Ang* 1F **51**
Trinity. *Edin* 2E **33**
Trislaig. *High* 4D **55**
Trochry. *Per* 3E **49**
Trondavoe. *Shet* 4F **101**
**Troon**. *S Ayr* 2E **19**
Troqueer. *Dum* 4E **13**
Troutbeck. *Cumb* 4C **8**
Trumaisgearraidh. *W Isl* 5C **94**
Trumpan. *High* 3B **72**
Tughall. *Nmbd* 3F **25**
Tulchan. *Per* 1E **41**
Tullibardine. *Per* 2E **41**
Tullibody. *Clac* 4D **41**
Tullich. *Arg* 2B **38**
Tullich. *High* 1C **64**
(nr. Lochcarron)
Tullich. *High* 2F **77**
(nr. Tain)
Tullich. *Mor* 1E **69**
Tullich Muir. *High* 2E **77**
Tulliemet. *Per* 2E **49**
Tulloch. *Abers* 2D **71**
Tulloch. *High* 4B **84**
(nr. Bonar Bridge)
Tulloch. *High* 3A **56**
(nr. Fort William)
Tulloch. *High* 4A **68**
(nr. Grantown-on-Spey)
Tulloch. *Per* 1F **41**
Tullochgorm. *Arg* 4A **38**
Tullybeagles Lodge.
*Per* 4F **49**
Tullymurdoch. *Per* 2B **50**
Tullynessle. *Abers* 4A **70**
Tummel Bridge. *Per* 2C **48**
Tunga. *W Isl* 3F **97**
Turfholm. *S Lan* 2D **21**
Turnberry. *S Ayr* 1D **11**
Turnhouse. *Edin* 2D **33**
Turriff. *Abers* 1C **70**
Turtory. *Mor* 1A **70**
Tushielaw. *Bord* 4C **22**
Twatt. *Orkn* 1A **98**
Twatt. *Shet* 1B **100**
Twechar. *E Dun* 2E **31**
Tweedbank. *Bord* 2E **23**
Tweedmouth. *Nmbd* 4F **35**
Tweedsmuir. *Bord* 3F **21**
Twynholm. *Dum* 2B **6**
Tyndrum. *Stir* 4E **47**
Tynehead. *Midl* 4F **33**
Tyninghame. *E Lot* 2C **34**
Tynron. *Dum* 2D **13**
Tyrie. *Abers* 3E **81**

## U

Uachdar. *W Isl* 2H **93**
Uags. *High* 2A **64**
Uddingston. *S Lan* 3E **31**
Uddington. *S Lan* 2D **21**
Udny Green. *Abers* 3D **71**
Udny Station. *Abers* 3E **71**
Udston. *S Lan* 4E **31**
Udstonhead. *S Lan* 1C **20**
Ugadale. *Arg* 3E **17**
Uidh. *W Isl* 3B **92**
Uig. *Arg* 2G **91**
**Uig**. *High* 3C **72**
(nr. Balgown)
Uig. *High* 4A **72**
(nr. Dunvegan)
Uigshader. *High* 1D **63**
Uisken. *Arg* 2A **36**
Ulbster. *High* 3C **90**
Uldale. *Cumb* 4B **8**
**Ullapool**. *High* 4C **82**
Ullinish. *High* 2C **62**
Ullock. *Cumb* 4F **7**
Ulsta. *Shet* 3G **101**
Ulva House. *Arg* 4B **44**
Unapool. *High* 4D **87**
Underhoull. *Shet* 1H **101**
Unthank. *Cumb* 3C **8**
(nr. Carlisle)
Unthank. *Cumb* 3F **9**
(nr. Gamblesby)
Unthank. *Cumb* 4D **9**
(nr. Penrith)
Unthank End. *Cumb* 4D **9**
Uphall. *W Lot* 2C **32**
Uphall Station. *W Lot* 2C **32**
Uplawmoor. *E Ren* 4C **30**
Uppat. *High* 3D **85**
Upper Badcall. *High* 3C **86**
Upper Bighouse. *High* 2D **89**
Upper Boddam. *Abers* 2B **70**
Upper Bogside. *Mor* 4D **79**
Upper Boyndlie. *Abers* 3E **81**
Upper Cuttlehill. *Abers* 1F **69**
Upper Dallachy. *Mor* 3E **79**
Upper Derraid. *High* 2B **68**
Upper Diabaig. *High* 3B **74**
Upper Dochcarty. *High* 3C **76**
Upper Dounreay. *High* 1E **89**
Upper Gills. *High* 5B **98**
Upper Glenfintaig. *High* 3F **55**
Upper Hindhope. *Bord* 4A **24**
Upper Kirkton. *Abers* 2C **70**
Upper Kirkton. *N Ayr* 4F **29**
Upper Knockando. *Mor* 1C **68**
Upper Knockchoilum. *High* 4B **66**
Upper Largo. *Fife* 3D **43**
Upper Latheron. *High* 4A **90**
Upper Lenie. *High* 3C **66**
Upper Lochton. *Abers* 2B **60**
Upper Lybster. *High* 4B **90**
Upper Milovaig. *High* 1A **62**
Upper Neepaback.
*Shet* 3H **101**
Upper Ollach. *High* 2E **63**
Upper Rusko. *Dum* 1A **6**
Upper Sandaig. *High* 4A **64**
Upper Sanday. *Orkn* 2D **98**
Upper Skelmorlie. *N Ayr* 3F **29**
Upper Sonachan. *Arg* 1B **38**
Upper Tillyrie. *Per* 3A **42**
Uppertown. *High* 5B **98**
Uppertown. *Orkn* 3C **98**
Upper Urquhart. *Fife* 3A **42**
Upsettlington. *Bord* 1B **24**
Upton. *Cumb* 4C **8**
Urafirth. *Shet* 4F **101**
Uragaig. *Arg* 4A **36**
Urchany. *High* 1F **67**
Ure. *Shet* 4E **101**
Urgha. *W Isl* 3F **95**
Urquhart. *Mor* 3D **79**
Urray. *High* 4C **76**
Usan. *Ang* 2F **51**
Uyeasound. *Shet* 1H **101**

## V

Valsgarth. *Shet* 1H **101**
Valtos. *High* 3E **73**
Vatsetter. *Shet* 3H **101**
Vatten. *High* 1B **62**
Vaul. *Arg* 3F **91**
Veensgarth. *Shet* 2C **100**
Veness. *Orkn* 5G **99**
Vidlin. *Shet* 5G **101**
**Viewpark**. *N Lan* 3F **31**
Voe. *Shet* 5G **101**
(nr. Hillside)
Voe. *Shet* 3F **101**
(nr. Swinister)

Published by Geographers' A-Z Map Company Limited
An imprint of HarperCollins Publishers
Westerhill Road
Bishopbriggs
Glasgow
G64 2QT

HarperCollinsPublishers
Macken House, 39/40 Mayor Street Upper, Dublin 1, D01 C9W8, Ireland
www.az.co.uk
a-z.maps@harpercollins.co.uk

3rd edition 2020

© Collins Bartholomew Ltd 2020

This product uses map data licenced from Ordnance Survey
© Crown copyright and database rights 2022 OS 100018598

AZ, A-Z and AtoZ are registered trademarks of Geographers' A-Z Map Company Limited

MIX
Paper from
responsible sources
FSC™ C007454